Prospect Research

Books by Mathew Iredale

The Problem of Free Will, a contemporary introduction
Prospecting for Benefactors: How to find major donors to support your school
Prospecting for Philanthropists: How to find major donors to support your charity

Prospect Research

How to find major donors to support *your* charity

MATHEW IREDALE

Copyright © 2019 Mathew Iredale

The moral rights of the author have been asserted.

All rights reserved. No part of this publication may be reproduced, distributed, or transmitted in any form or by any means, including photocopying, recording, or other electronic or mechanical methods, without the prior written permission of the publisher, except in the case of brief quotations embodied in critical reviews and certain other non-commercial uses permitted by copyright law.

British Library Cataloguing-in-Publication Data
A catalogue record for this book is available from the British Library.

ISBN: 9781795047104

Designed and typeset in Garamond.

To Freddie and Emily

Contents

Chapter 1	**Introduction**	1
Chapter 2	**Why support *your* charity?**	
	2.1 Donor motivation	4
	2.2 Affinity & passion	6
	2.3 Personal connection	11
	2.4 Location	12
	2.5 Personal impact	14
	2.6 Worthiness	16
	2.7 Conclusion	18
Chapter 3	**Data Protection**	
	3.1 Data Protection Principles	22
	3.2 Purposes of processing	23
	3.3 Is the processing fair?	25
	3.4 Is the processing transparent?	38
	3.5 Is the processing lawful?	41
	3.6 Is the processing adequate?	45
	3.7 Is the data you hold accurate?	47
	3.8 Is the processing secure?	50
	3.9 Next steps	51
Chapter 4	**That thing you do**	54
Chapter 5	**Digging into your database**	
	5.1 Past major donors	59
	5.2 Private banks	62
	5.3 Occupation	65
	5.4 Email addresses	67
	5.5 Property	68
	5.6 Titles	70
	5.7 Wealth screening	71

	5.8 DIY data screening	72
	5.9 Conclusion	73
Chapter 6	**Widening the search**	
	6.1 Competitor analysis	76
	6.2 Who's Who	79
	6.3 Local people	81
	6.4 Trustees & donors' networks	83
	6.5 Conclusion	86
Chapter 7	**Qualification**	
	7.1 Qualification as triage	89
	7.2 Google and Bing	91
	7.3 Companies House	95
	7.4 LinkedIn	101
	7.5 Property value	102
	7.6 Biographies	103
	7.7 Trustees of charitable trusts	104
	7.8 Other philanthropy	106
	7.9 News archives	108
	7.10 Due diligence	109
	7.11 Other resources	113
	7.12 Troubleshooting	117
	7.13 Conclusion	119
Chapter 8	**Preparing for cultivation**	
	8.1 Gift capacity	122
	8.2 Inclination	130
	8.3 Cultivation profiles	134
	8.4 Conclusion	140

Appendix – Privacy Statement

Acknowledgements

About the Author

Explanatory Preface

This book is an almost exact copy of my 2018 publication, *Prospecting for Philanthropists*. The reason for re-issuing it under a new name is simple: under the old name, it did not appear in Amazon searches of prospect research books, making it difficult to find, and so very few people had heard of it. A re-issue under the rather bland, but accurate, title *Prospect Research* is the obvious way to redress this.

As with the previous edition, I have taken the opportunity to review all the websites, updating them where necessary, and tweaked the text where I felt it could be improved.

1

Introduction

The purpose of this book is to enable you – to empower you – to find people who are capable of supporting your charity with a major gift.

What is a major gift? This really depends upon the size of your appeal, but generally speaking, a major gift is any donation that makes a significant difference to your charity. For some appeals this will be a gift of £25,000 or more, for others it will be a gift of £500 or less. Either way, the principals involved in identifying prospective major donors, or prospects, are the same.

My motivation in writing this book is very simple. There are a great many books about major gift fundraising, and how to run a capital campaign, but they all share the same basic shortcomings. First, they generally devote one chapter to identifying potential major donors when this is a subject to which one can devote a whole book (you're holding it in your hand right now) and second, the advice they provide is invariably long on theory and short on the practical steps you actually need to take.

This book is different.

Prospect Research

It offers tried and tested techniques from someone who has spent many years finding major gift prospects for local and national charities, hospitals, museums, theatres, schools and other charitable organisations, who appreciates the problems you will face when trying to identify them, and who knows the solutions. In this book I will show you how to find wealthy people who are willing and able to support *your* charity with a major gift.

To find major gift prospects you need to employ a set of techniques called prospect research. Prospect research involves identifying and then researching major gift prospects and is the vital component in the first and second stages of the overall process known as major gift fundraising:

1. **Identification** – the stage at which you first identify major gift prospects who may want to support your charity from amongst the much larger group of potential donors.

2. **Qualification** – the process by which you decide how good each prospect actually is, based upon their ability and inclination to support you with a major gift, which tells you who to approach first and for what level of donation (and who to disregard).

3. **Cultivation** – the stage at which you make contact with the prospect and try to engage them in your charity and its work.

4. **Solicitation** – the critical stage at which you ask the prospect for a donation and thank them for their support.

5. **Stewardship** – the stage at which you continue to strengthen your relationship with them, in appreciation of what they have done and in the hope they will wish to support you again.

In this book, I will take you step by step through the first two stages: identification and qualification. By the end you will be in possession of a list of prospects ready to be cultivated for a major gift in support of *your* charity.

Along the way you will discover what will motivate potential major donors to support your charity (chapter 2), how to carry out research in accordance with data protection legislation (chapter 3), the importance of matching the interests of your prospects with specific areas of your work (chapter 4), the numerous techniques you can use to identify prospects (chapters 5 & 6), and the best research resources to qualify and rank your prospects (chapters 7 & 8), so that you know who in your prospect pool to solicit first for a major gift and who to leave until later.

2

Why support *your* charity?

2.1 Donor motivation

Why would someone want to give *your* charity a major gift? This is the question you need to answer if you are to successfully solicit major gifts. And you will need to come up with a better answer than 'because we're a great charity!' There are lots of great charities – thousands and thousands of them, in fact – all of them vying for the attention of philanthropists. I know of one philanthropist who receives several charitable requests *per day*. That's over 500 requests per year. And I doubt that he is that unusual.

If you really want to understand why a philanthropist might want to support your charity over the other 499 vying for their attention each year, you need to understand major donor motivation. I'm not talking about a donor's motives for giving you a small donation. That may be for any one of a variety of reasons, both rational and irrational (see Beth Breeze's seminal study, *How Donors Choose Charities*, for a discussion of the various different ways in which

Chapter 2 Why support *your* charity?

donors explain their support of a particular charity). I'm talking about major donations. It is only when you really understand what someone's motives are for giving a large donation *to your charity* that you can appreciate just who will be attracted to it and who it is you should be looking for when trying to identify major gift prospects.

Luckily for us, over the last 10 to 15 years there have been a fair number of studies which either looked explicitly at what motivates philanthropists to give, or in which motivation is considered as part of a wider remit.

One of the first studies to explicitly look at the reasons why the rich give to charity is in many ways the most interesting. Published in 2002 by the Institute for Public Policy Research and based on interviews with 56 people, the study, *A bit rich? What the wealthy think about giving*, looked at the various reasons why wealthy donors support charities but, just as importantly, it also looked at the different reasons why some wealthy people *never* support charities (except perhaps to throw a few coins in a collecting tin). Most fascinatingly, the author of the study, Laura Edwards, came to the conclusion that "not giving to charity is the default option." She continues, "Giving is not passive, it requires action and involvement when it moves away from the dropping of spare coins in a collecting tin on a shop counter." And how can you encourage someone if not giving is the default option?

This research shows that there are key factors that, if in place, are *more likely* to lead to the individual engaging with the cause and deciding to give their time or money.

A conclusion which has been confirmed by all subsequent research into major gift motivation. Let us now take a look at this research and the key factors which it has uncovered.

2.2 Affinity & passion

Published in 2004, Theresa Lloyd's book *Why Rich People Give* was the result of the first major study in the UK into the attitudes of major donors (the earlier study by Edwards only asked wealthy donors about their giving, rather than major gifts). Through interviews with 76 millionaires (with a net worth ranging from a few million pounds to over £500m) and a further 24 volunteer fundraising leaders/askers and professional advisors (many of whom were also wealthy), it provided an in-depth analysis of the motivations that prompt the wealthy to support charities.

What Lloyd found was that the key motivational factor for the majority of people is a passion for the cause:

> For many, a passion for a specific cause is inseparable from motivation; the enthusiasm underpins and is reinforced by the affinity for and relationship with the individual organisations which focus on the subjects of concern to the donor. Donors who care deeply about a generic

Chapter 2 Why support *your* charity?

cause, whether child poverty or opera, may well support more than one charity or institution addressing those issues.

It is a finding echoed by the report *Philanthropic Lives, The unique experiences of eight UK philanthropists* published in 2011 by New Philanthropy Capital. The report concludes that the "most successful philanthropists also seem to be those who align their giving with their passion."

There are several reasons why someone may have a passion for a particular cause, but by far and away the most common and powerful one is that the person has had some personal experience that is directly related to that cause.

This was one of the key findings in a study published in 2007 by Ipsos MORI, *Charitable Giving by Wealthy People*. Based on 44 in-depth interviews with "a range of wealthy individuals", the study looked at the giving behaviour of wealthy people, their awareness of tax efficient giving, and what motivated them to give to charity.

The study found that personal affiliation to a charity was often founded on a long-term relationship with the charity, "sometimes arising from a family illness or other experience." One of the donors had the following to say about the motivational factors that lie behind support of a particular cause:

> 'Well it's normally because either you yourself have been involved in raising money for them, or because you've got a very strong personal, family,

emotional attachment to something. I mean why would I give something like that to [local charity]? Well my father was a much decorated first gunboat captain in the Second World War and was killed in the second world war so that's something I feel very strongly I wish to support.'

"The question of what leads people to give to one type of charity but inhibits them giving to another," noted Laura Edwards "is too big to cover within this research." But this was precisely the question that Beth Breeze asked in her ground-breaking study, *How donors choose charities*. Breeze interviewed 60 committed donors (all were Charities Aid Foundation account holders) representing a spread of gender, age and income levels. Breeze found that a donor's charitable outlook is acquired as a result of life-long processes and their decisions about who to support are often closely related to earlier life experiences. "Examples of autobiographical factors behind giving decisions came up frequently in the interviews," she concludes. Typical high-income donor responses included the following:

'My son had meningitis so I give to the Meningitis Trust; he was in the intensive care unit at the Royal Berkshire Hospital so I give to the intensive care unit there. It's about personal experience really.'

'A number of my friends have died of cancer and they've had enormous help from Marie Curie, so I would definitely respond to them.'

Chapter 2 Why support *your* charity?

'I support the British Heart Foundation since I had a quadruple bypass myself.'

'My father had heart disease which is why I support the Heart Foundation, and my aunt worked for animal welfare charities all her life, so that's one of the reasons I support dogs' homes and things like that. It all comes down to your own experiences, doesn't it?'

Breeze concludes that "on the whole people draw on their own life experiences to create what have been called 'philanthropic autobiographies'. People give to causes that they feel some connection to, or affinity with, as a result of experiences and incidents that occur in their personal and professional lives."

In her study for the Institute for Public Policy Research, Laura Edwards also found that donors "frequently describe giving to charities that are close to their heart."

It is not surprising that medical charities come high on the list of major charities in the UK. Most people at some point in their lives will come into contact with ill-health; either their own or that of friends or family. Such first-hand experience serves as a powerful and direct message that the work of charities in a particular area is important.

She noted the following responses:

'My partner's mother died of cancer and it is only since going out with her that I have actually started to think more about giving to cancer charities.'

'I think you give to things that have touched your own life, where there's a personal connection...I give to the Royal National Institute for the Blind because a friend of mine has a son who's blind and we're also keen to support HIV charities because a friend of ours died of AIDS.'

In *My Philanthropy*, published in 2013 by New Philanthropy Capital, "nineteen high-profile individuals introduce the charities they feel most passionate about." Each of the interviews confirmed the importance of personal experience in underlying someone's passion for a particular cause. Belfast-born Harvey McGrath of the hedge fund Man Group is a supporter of The Integrated Education Fund in Northern Ireland. "Those of us who have experience of Northern Ireland feel passionately that one issue you have to address is generational change, and you do this by bringing kids together at an early age."

Baroness Martha Lane Fox is a dotcom entrepreneur and trustee of Reprieve, which gives legal representation to people facing the death penalty. "I've always been passionate about prisons. I watched a documentary on Feltham when I was very young that had a huge influence on me—I also hate small spaces!"

For Baroness Julia Neuberger, former CEO of the King's Fund, it was her mother's experience which was central to her philanthropic autobiography:

'I feel most passionate about the charity we set up in memory of my parents—the Walter and Liesel Schwab Charitable Trust. It's there to support

Chapter 2 Why support *your* charity?

young refugees and asylum seekers to get access to education. My mother came to this country as a Jewish refugee from Nazi Germany and she got lots of help from a whole variety of people of all faiths and backgrounds.'

But passion for a cause with which your charity is concerned will not necessarily translate into support for *your* charity, especially if there are other charities that represent the same cause. To go from general passion to specific support often requires one or more other motivational factors to be fulfilled.

2.3 Personal connection

One powerful motivating factor for persuading someone to support *your* charity as opposed to another with a similar cause is a personal connection – a friendship or, at the very least, an acquaintance – between that person and someone who works for your charity or who already supports it.

According to Laura Edwards, "With wealthy potential donors the approach may make or break their decision to give; particularly important is who does the asking…Frequently they described getting involved with a particular charity through a friend."

Theresa Lloyd found that "Virtually everyone interviewed will at least review and respond to a request that comes from a person or organisation they know and respect…If the asker has given money, so much the better; several people alluded to this." Typical donor responses included the following:

> 'The friend as endorser is crucial because the friend has invested personal capital – time and emotion – so I will help.'

> 'A second major factor is where people I know are asking for money. It's about respect, and their involvement endorses the cause and the relationship.'

Similarly, Beth Breeze found that people support charities when they have a personal relationship with someone in that charity:

> 'I do support some very small charities through personal contact…There's one that's run by two people I know.'

> 'We give regularly to a charity where we know the individual who's involved in running it…we try to support him in the way that we can.'

And the Ipsos MORI study concluded that "Across all donor groups, there were feelings of obligation to donate relatively large amounts in sponsorship to friends, family or colleagues when they may not necessarily have donated to that particular charity otherwise."

2.4 Location

Another strong motivational factor is being asked for support by a charity that is local to the donor. According to the Ipsos MORI study "Local charities were also particularly important to participants as they report a feeling of personal responsibility to support these causes."

Breeze also reports locality as being a powerful motivating factor. The following response is typical of many:

> 'I think people do relate more locally. There are hospices everywhere but somehow in your own backyard you can relate to it. Like in football, generally you support your local team.'

In 2011, New Philanthropy Capital and Coutts published the report *Inspiring local philanthropy* specifically on the subject of supporting local charities. According to Marcelle Speller, founder of Localgiving.com, "Local philanthropy gives me a sense of community, of belonging, and it recharges me. You can see that you are giving effectively, and have the most joyous, enriching experiences." This viewpoint was echoed by the philanthropists interviewed, such as the entrepreneur Peter Saunders, founder of The Peter Saunders Trust:

> 'The great thing about giving locally is that you have intimate knowledge of that area. This means that you can select what you fund wisely, get involved with the causes and influence what happens with the funding. I like the whole sense of involvement. I get a lot of pleasure out of making things happen, guiding people, stepping in if things are not going well, and actually seeing the benefits.'

A similar view was expressed by David Laing, chairman of The Kirby Laing Foundation:

> 'Local giving is important because you can focus funds to have the greatest effect. Rather than being sector specific, we are able to focus on a geographic area, supporting a wide range of projects. If you compare giving locally with nationally or internationally there is a completely different level of reward. I enjoy giving to a local charity. You feel much closer to it, and you're more likely to see the result of a gift or indeed a gift in kind.'

David Laing's last point brings us neatly to the next motivational factor.

2.5 Personal impact

The extent to which someone's donation will make a difference to a charity is a strong motivational factor. Donors are more attracted to a charity if they believe that their donation will have a demonstrable impact.

Personal impact was identified by Theresa Lloyd as being one of the primary motivational factors: "[e]ven if the cause is one which the donor supports in principle, the determining factor is the donor's conviction that the gift will make a difference." She found that many donors admitted they were reluctant to fund core costs, seeing this more as the responsibility of institutional grant-makers or the government. They would much prefer to fund a project that shows how their gift will impact upon the

Chapter 2 Why support *your* charity?

charity and make a significant difference to its work rather than add to the general donation pool, especially where a larger charity is concerned. For this reason, some donors prefer to give to smaller charities, where their large donations have a clear and long-term difference, or support individuals working in a particular field, where the impact of their donation can clearly be seen. Related to this, when donors were asked whether they regretted any of the donations they had made, one of the most consistently cited responses was a lack of confidence that their donation had made any difference.

Personal impact was also identified as a motivational factor by the Ipsos MORI study: "For small committed donors this could involve sponsoring a child and receiving letters on that child's progress, while for larger donors this may involve helping with the maintenance or re-building of their local church."

Beth Breeze also found that "a desire for personal impact influences donors' selection of charitable recipients." Like Lloyd, she found that some high-income donors prefer to support smaller charities:

> One donor supports a small local theatre because his donation 'makes a significant difference', whereas he feels that giving the same amount to a national theatre would mean 'it would get drowned out.' Another described donating to a 'very small charity' because 'it means a huge lot to give them even £100.' Reflecting on the attractions of smaller charities, an interviewee

explained: 'We didn't really want to support things where we felt our contribution was negligible.'

This is not to say that major donors will not support large charities – of course they do – but larger charities will need to make more of an effort than small charities to show how significant donations really make a difference to their work. Larger charities in particular may need to provide specific projects that show how a donor's major gift will impact upon the charity and make a significant difference to its work rather than become lost in the much larger pool of smaller donations.

2.6 Worthiness

An easily overlooked motivational factor identified by the Ipsos MORI study is the perceived 'worthiness' of a charity. Worthiness in this sense does not just mean whether your charity's cause is worthy of support – one person's worthy cause is another person's pointless exercise – but rather it relates to such things as "Charity overheads, excessive bureaucracy and levels of staff competency" all of which were highlighted by Ipsos MORI as particular issues related to how worthy a charity was perceived to be, especially "large salaries for chief executives and hidden administrative fees."

The suspicion that some charities are excessively bureaucratic and inefficient was also noted in the 2009 study by Barclays Wealth, *Tomorrow's Philanthropist*.

Chapter 2 Why support *your* charity?

Barclays commissioned an in-depth survey of 500 US and UK philanthropists. The survey was the largest of its kind at the time and looked at the future of giving and the effect the economic downturn was having on wealthy donors around the world. In 2010, a brief follow-up report was published, *Barriers to giving*, which discussed some of the reasons why the rich do not give more to charity. Some of these barriers are beyond the control of individual charities (such as the state of the economy and the level of taxation), but one of the barriers clearly is within a charity's control:

> [T]he majority of the wealthy (53%) believe that charities are inefficient in managing donations. Men are more sceptical than women and the very wealthy the most sceptical. 65% of UK-based ultra high net worth individuals (those with over £3m in investable assets) believe charities are inefficient.

In other words, you will be more attractive to philanthropists if you can show you are not inefficient, excessively bureaucratic, with incompetent and highly paid staff and large administrative costs. How you go about proving this is down to you, but it is a very important first step to realise that your charity and its finances, objectives, and impact upon the field in which you work, will be scrutinised closely by many, if not all, potential major donors. Can you justify the salaries of your highest paid staff? Do you know how much of the money you receive in donations goes towards administration and how much to the actual cause – and are these figures acceptable? Do you measure the impact that your work has? That is to say, do you have in place a set of procedures through which your charity can determine what difference its work makes?

Impact measurement in particular is becoming increasingly important to some rich donors. In a survey of charities by New Philanthropy Capital (*Making an Impact*, 2012), when asked why they had increased their efforts to measure the impact that their work has, more than half the charities answered that it was because donors increasingly required it. Take note.

2.7 Conclusion

You should now have a good idea of what motivates rich people. They are more likely to support *your* charity if,

1. They care about the cause with which your charity is involved.
2. They, or one of their family or close friends, had a personal experience which either brought them into direct contact with your charity or prompted them to have a particular affinity with your charity.
3. They know someone who works for your charity or who is already a major donor to your charity.
4. They grew up in, or now live or work in, an area in which your charity operates.

Chapter 2 Why support *your* charity?

5. They know their gift will really make a difference to your work; that it will have a clear *impact* on your work.
6. They regard your charity as worthy of support; it is not inefficient, excessively bureaucratic, with incompetent or over-paid staff.

Of these six motivational factors, the first four will lead us directly to the sort of rich people who will be attracted to your charity and want to support it with a significant gift. Once you have identified these people, you then need to make sure that your charity is up to the mark with regard to the last two motivational factors. It will undo all your hard work if, having identified a number of rich people who ought to be attracted to your charity, they actually decide their gift will not make an appreciable difference or your charity is too inefficient or incompetent to be worthy of their support.

Wealth Reports

A bit rich? What the wealthy think about giving (The Institute for Public Policy Research, 2002).

Why Rich People Give by Theresa Lloyd (Association of Charitable Foundations, 2004. Lloyd and Beth Breeze have recently co-authored an updated edition, *Richer Lives, why rich people give*, Directory of Social Change, 2013)

Charitable Giving by Wealthy People (Ipsos MORI, 2007).

Wealth and Philanthropy: the views of those who advise the rich (Philanthropy UK, 2007).

Women & Philanthropy: inspiring women, inspired giving (Philanthropy UK, 2008).

Natural Philanthropists: Findings of the Family Business Philanthropy and Social Responsibility Inquiry (Institute for Family Business and Community Foundation Network, 2009)

Tomorrow's Philanthropist (Barclays Wealth, 2009)

How donors choose charities (Centre for Charitable Giving and Philanthropy, 2010)

Barriers to giving (Barclays Wealth, 2010)

Family philanthropy: rewards and challenges (New Philanthropy Capital, 2010)

Philanthropic Lives, The unique experiences of eight UK philanthropists (New Philanthropy Capital, 2011)

Inspiring local philanthropy (New Philanthropy Capital and Coutts, 2011)

Making an Impact (New Philanthropy Capital, 2012)

My Philanthropy (New Philanthropy Capital, 2013)

3

Data protection

3.1 The Data Protection Principles

As soon as you start to process personal data, even something as simple as adding someone's name and address to a spreadsheet, you are subject to data protection legislation. Specifically, the Privacy and Electronic Communications Regulations from 2003 and the General Data Protection Regulation (GDPR) from 2018. (There is also a Data Protection Act 2018, but as its function is to add some UK-specific provisions to the GDPR, none of which are that relevant to prospect research, we can safely ignore it and focus solely on the GDPR.)

In this chapter I wish to take you through the main principles of the GDPR, explaining what you can and cannot do when researching people.

Article 5 of the GDPR, states that data must be:

- processed lawfully, fairly & transparently
- processed in a manner compatible with, and relevant to, the purpose of its collection
- adequate, relevant and limited to what is necessary to process it

Chapter 3 Data protection

- kept accurate, up to date and for no longer than is necessary
- processed safely and securely

As far as prospect research is concerned, what this means is that when processing someone's data, you need to consider the following questions:

1. What are the purposes of the processing?
2. Is the processing fair?
3. Is the processing transparent?
4. Is the processing lawful?
5. Is the processing limited to what is adequate, relevant and necessary?
6. Is the data we hold accurate, up to date and held for no longer than is necessary?
7. Is the processing safe and secure?

3.2 What is the purpose of the processing?

Article 5(b) states:

> Personal data shall be collected for specified, explicit and legitimate purposes and not further processed in a manner that is incompatible with those purposes.

Recital 39 adds:

> In particular, the specific purposes for which personal data are processed should be explicit and legitimate and determined at the time of the collection of the personal data.

According to Tim Turner, a data protection consultant who used to work for the Information Commissioners Office (ICO), and author of the guide *Fundraising and data protection*, we cannot just say "fundraising purposes" and leave it at that:

> The discipline of clearly identifying your purposes at the outset is one of the most useful things you can do, and you must break down 'fundraising purposes' into its constituent parts.

Your charity should already have a list of purposes for which it processes data (e.g. to maintain a list of donors, to claim gift aid, to update supporters about your work, and so on) but you also need to list those purposes which specifically relate to major gift fundraising and prospect research). E.g.,

- We use information our supporters have given us voluntarily (e.g. where they live, who they bank with, what their occupation is) to identify wealthy supporters on our database who may wish to support our work with a major gift.

- We use information that is already in the public domain (information that has been published in print or online) to identify wealthy individuals who may be interested in supporting our work with a major gift.

- We use information that is already in the public domain (information that has been published in print or online) to identify wealthy individuals who may be known to our existing major donors.

Chapter 3 Data protection

- We use information that is already in the public domain (information that has been published in print or online) to carry out due diligence checks on all new major donors.

- We use information that is already in the public domain (information that has been published in print or online) to ensure that the information we have on our major donors is accurate and up to date.

Once you have listed your purposes, you then need to ensure, first, that you do not process data in a manner that is incompatible with those purposes and secondly, that you make these purposes easily accessible to anyone whose data you may be processing. According to the ICO, the most obvious way to do this is through a "privacy notice" given to individuals at the time their personal data is collected. This is discussed in more detail in Section 3.4, on transparency.

3.3 Is the processing fair?

Article 5(a) of the GDPR states that data must be "processed lawfully, fairly and in a transparent manner." I will be considering transparency in the next section, and lawfulness after that, but for this section I wish to look at fairness.

In their Feb 2017 paper, *Fundraising and regulatory compliance*, the ICO states "Processing does not become fair just because you tell the person it will happen." They continue:

> An individual's reasonable expectations are part of the assessment of whether you are processing personal information fairly. This assessment is separate from the requirement to be transparent with individuals about what you're doing with their personal information and why.

We may be able to learn a great deal about someone from their Facebook profile (their friends, their family, what they look like, where they holiday, their likes and interests, and so on), but even if we say in our policy statement that we use Facebook, is it ethical to be using what is for many people a very *private* medium? After all, many people are still not aware of how easy it is to search their Facebook profile if they do not make it private.

In short, as well as asking whether we *can* do something under the GDPR we must ask ourselves *should* we be doing it? And for a very good reason, says Tim Turner:

> If challenged, either by the subjects, by the Information Commissioner or the courts, you will need to set how you have dealt with fairness. It will be much harder to do this if you have not thought about it in advance.

With this in mind, in the following section I set out the six reasons why I believe it *is* ethically fair for a charity to research potential major donors.

Chapter 3 Data protection

3.3.1 Major donors expect it

There are three arguments to be made for believing that major donors expect charities to carry out research into them.

The first is anecdotal. My twenty years' experience in researching and fundraising from major donors tells me that most of them expect charities to carry out research into them, their wealth, and their philanthropy, before approaching them for a donation. The most obvious proof of this is the profiles I've been sent by donors themselves (and also, on occasion, profiles of the guests they are bringing to an event). I've also had numerous conversations with donors and prospects in the last few years when I've discussed the work I do (e.g. checking company annual reports or newspaper reports for information about the prospect). Not one of them has *ever* expressed any concerns about this and several of them clearly found it fascinating.

The second argument is the existence of philanthropists' personal websites which specifically highlight their careers and philanthropy (especially if they have a charitable foundation). To suggest it would not be fair to research such people when many have intentionally and explicitly made this information publicly available would be ridiculous. Such websites have clearly been created, in part, to facilitate prospect research; to enable fundraisers to know which charities and causes the philanthropist supports and why.

Prospect Research

The third and most powerful argument is the research carried out by Beth Breeze and Theresa Lloyd. They interviewed some 80 major donors and published the results in their book *Richer Lives, why rich people give*. Amongst many interesting findings was the following:

> Donors feel that fundraising has become more professional over the past decade, especially in terms of the right research being conducted before approaches are made, and a better understanding of how different donors might want to engage with causes.

When they specifically asked how donors regard fundraisers, most donors agreed that fundraising had improved:

> The most significant area of perceived improvement (cited by 78% of those who agreed that fundraising has improved) was in better research before donors are approached.

Research is clearly seen as fundamental by many donors:

> ...inadequate or non-existent research not only wastes money, it makes the whole sector look unprofessional. Donors on the receiving end of 'bad asks' do not forget the experience, and may even redirect their irritation at the whole charity sector, rather than just the organisation that approached them.

Their conclusion is clear:

…better donor research is cited as the most significant area of improvement in fundraising over the past decade.

If you are still unsure, then why not ask your existing major donors (or your largest or warmest donors)? What level of research do they expect you to carry out?

3.3.2 It enables more effective and efficient targeting of communications

Carrying out research into potential major donors before approaching them greatly increases the likelihood that the charity will only approach those donors who are willing and able to support it with a major gift. If this research shows that a person is unlikely to be interested in making a major gift, or that they are unlikely to be able to, the charity won't contact them for a major gift.

It's as simple as that.

All of which enables the charity to raise funds more cost-effectively than it would otherwise, allowing it to devote more money to its services.

3.3.3 It prevents reputational risk to the charity

A responsible charity *must* carry out research into its potential major donors to protect against significant damage to the charity's reputation arising from accepting a large gift from someone with a genuine conflict of interests with that charity.

This significant damage goes much further than a few awkward headlines in a newspaper. Accepting a major gift from the wrong donor could lead to:

- The loss of donations from other supporters equivalent to or greater than the value of the major gift.
- The loss of volunteers whose services could be of equivalent value to the gift.
- The loss of staff or the inability to recruit staff with the necessary skills and dedication.

Consider the damage that could arise for a cancer charity that accepts a large donation from the Managing Director of a cigarette company; an animal rights charity that accepts a large donation from a staunch supporter of fox-hunting, or a child welfare charity which accepts a large donation from the Chief Executive of a company which employs child labour in Asia.

A charity has a duty to its other donors, its volunteers, its staff and its beneficiaries, to guard against reputational risk by checking the background of prospective major donors through prospect research.

3.3.4 We only use non-intrusive sources of public information

As stated in the list of purposes earlier, and as you will see in chapter 7, prospect research should be carried out using non-intrusive publicly available sources of

Chapter 3 Data protection

information. These sources include Companies House, the electoral register, the phone book, the Charity Commission's Register of Charities, Who's Who, LinkedIn, company annual reports and articles in newspapers and magazines. These sources are all known and recognised as containing information which is readily and freely available to anyone who wishes to use it. For this reason, I do not consider the use of these sources to be intrusive (and nor, I am sure, would the majority of major donors).

In contrast to this, there are certain sources, which although they are technically publicly available, I believe would be intrusive to use for fundraising purposes. Sources such as Facebook, Twitter, JustGiving, the Land Registry, online planning applications, or websites that are similar to these. My recommendation is that you do not use these websites to carry out prospect research. I think you would find it much more difficult to justify their use to the ICO than the non-intrusive sources above.

In taking this position I am being mindful of the ICO's own guidance from their document *Fundraising and regulatory compliance*:

> ...individuals may want as many people as possible to read their tweet or Facebook post. Yet that doesn't mean they're agreeing to have those pieces of information collected and analysed to set (say) their insurance premium or their credit risk. The fact that personal information is publicly available doesn't make it 'fair game'. And

it doesn't make further use of that personal information for any purpose fair.

The ICO's guidance continues:

"When obtaining and using publicly available personal information, you must ensure you're getting and using it for specified and lawful purposes as required by Principle 2 of the DPA. Further, the purposes for which you intend to process the personal information must be compatible with the purposes for which its processing was originally intended. So when you are getting and intending to use this information, you must compare the original purpose for which it was collected and used against the purpose for which you intend to use it."

Similar wording is used in the GDPR (Recital 50):

The processing of personal data for purposes other than those for which the personal data were initially collected should be allowed only where the processing is compatible with the purposes for which the personal data were initially collected.

Note that both the ICO's current guidance and the GDPR state that the purposes for which you intend to process personal information must be compatible with the purposes for which its processing was originally intended and not *identical* to those purposes.

But how do you decide whether the two purposes are compatible? Article 6(4) lists the following criteria:

Chapter 3 Data protection

Where the processing for a purpose other than that for which the personal data have been collected is not based on the data subject's consent [such as using publicly available data] the controller shall, in order to ascertain whether processing for another purpose is compatible with the purpose for which the personal data are initially collected, take into account, inter alia:

(a) any link between the purposes for which the personal data have been collected and the purposes of the intended further processing;

(b) the context in which the personal data have been collected, in particular regarding the relationship between data subjects and the controller;

(c) the nature of the personal data, in particular whether special categories of personal data are processed;

(d) the possible consequences of the intended further processing for data subjects;

(e) the existence of appropriate safeguards, which may include encryption or pseudonymisation.

Again, note the wording used. It says we must "take into account" the five points listed and not that we *must* satisfy them all. Even so, it is reasonable to assume that the more of these criteria you do satisfy, or obviously take into account, the more likely it is that the ICO will accept that *your* processing is compatible with the purpose for which the personal data were originally collected.

More usefully, the ICO provides the following guidance:

> In deciding whether the two are compatible, you should consider things such as:
> - the individuals' reasonable expectations
> - the potential effect on them of the processing
> - what they've been told.

Let us consider each of these points in turn.

The individuals' reasonable expectations

We saw earlier in the chapter that it is the expectation of many major donors that we will research them, and given the easy availability of so much publicly available information, especially through a simple search of Google or Bing, it is entirely reasonable to assume they expect us to use this information when carrying out our research.

But it is just as reasonable, in my opinion, to assume that they do not expect us to use publicly available information which is clearly of a very personal or private nature. And this includes much of the information which people post on Facebook and twitter (and messages left on other websites, such as JustGiving and personal blogs). Whilst there are privacy settings on some of these websites, it is not reasonable to assume that just because the data subject has not used them, that they are happy for any and all information they post to be seen by a complete stranger, much less that it be used by a charity for fundraising purposes.

The potential effect on them of processing

The overall effect on the data subject of obtaining publicly available information about them to carry out prospect research will be either benign or beneficial.

As I stated above, researching potential major donors ensures that we are far more likely to only approach those people who are willing and able to support us with a major gift. Which also means we are far less likely to approach those who are not capable or willing.

What they've been told

The issue of what data subjects have been told about how we process their data is considered in detail in Section 3.4 on transparency.

In brief, it is recommended to fully disclose the publicly available sources we use for our research, both in an online policy statement and in a statement to the donor, as soon as it is reasonable to do so (e.g. when they are first contacted by letter or email to invite them to an event or to request a meeting).

3.3.5 All information collected is safe and secure.

All the information you collect must be held securely, either on a password protected database, or in documents or spreadsheets held on a password protected server, or, for paper files, in locked filing cabinets or drawers with adequate security to the room in which these are held.

Never pass prospects' data to third parties, unless it is in an encrypted form to a secure data processor which carries out data processing operations on your behalf.

And do ensure all staff who have access to your data are aware of their legal responsibilities under data protection laws.

The issue of safety and security is discussed in more detail in section 3.8.

3.3.6 It does not cause undue damage or distress to your donors

Recital 75 of the GDPR states:

> The risk to the rights and freedoms of natural persons, of varying likelihood and severity, may result from personal data processing which could lead to physical, material or non-material damage.

In particular, where the processing may give rise to "financial loss, damage to the reputation…or any other significant economic or social disadvantage" or where data subjects might be "prevented from exercising control over their personal data…" or where personal data are processed "which reveal racial or ethnic origin, political opinions, religion or philosophical beliefs…data concerning health or data concerning sex life or criminal convictions"

Recital 76 goes on to say:

Chapter 3 Data protection

The likelihood and severity of the risk to the rights and freedoms of the data subject should be determined by reference to the nature, scope, context and purposes of the processing. Risk should be evaluated on the basis of an objective assessment, by which it is established whether data processing operations involve a risk or a high risk.

If you carry out prospect research in the way described in this book then I believe there is no way it could cause a data subject damage or distress, either physically, financially, emotionally, or in any other noteworthy way and that there is little or no risk to the rights and freedoms of the data subject. What is more, we have very strong evidence that major donors *expect* charities to carry out research into them, so they clearly do not regard it as damaging or distressing.

In conclusion, in answer to the question 'Is the processing fair?' we can answer with an unequivocal 'yes' backed up by the following reasons:

1. Major donors expect it.
2. It enables more effective and efficient targeting of communications
3. It prevents reputational risk to the charity.
4. We only use non-intrusive sources of public information.
5. All information collected is safe and secure.
6. It does not cause undue damage or distress to your donors.

3.4 Is the processing transparent?

Recital 39 says:

> It should be transparent to natural persons that personal data concerning them are collected, used, consulted or otherwise processed and to what extent the personal data are or will be processed.

> The principle of transparency requires that any information and communication relating to the processing of those personal data be easily accessible and easy to understand, and that clear and plain language be used.

Adding to this, Recital 58 says:

> Such information could be provided in electronic form, for example, when addressed to the public, through a website.

Not only does the GDPR require us to be transparent in our data processing, but if you wish to use the Legitimate Interests justification for processing someone's data rather than consent (see Section 3.5) you must still provide them with the opportunity to object to this processing. This means you must be completely transparent about what you are doing with their data.

At the very least, this means you need a clear and easily accessible privacy statement on your website stating what sort of information you process and where you get the information. This is why it is vital that you list the purposes for which you process data (as I discussed in section 3.2).

But Article 12 goes further than this, I believe:

> The controller shall take appropriate measures to provide any information…relating to processing to the data subject in a concise, transparent, intelligible and easily accessible form, using clear and plain language.

Note the use of the phrase "easily accessible". A website privacy statement is clearly easily accessible to some, but it is also completely inaccessible to those who do not have online access. You should therefore also consider including a copy of your privacy statement with the first printed correspondence you send to a prospect. E.g. with an invitation to an event or the first time you send them a letter. If the first time you contact them is by email, you could include a link to the online privacy statement in the email. It should be clearly visible, so either just above or below your signature.

To quote data protection consultant Tim Turner again: "if you research people without telling them, it's a breach of DPA and GDPR." So you must provide your prospects with a privacy statement at the earliest opportunity. There is a sample privacy statement in the appendix to this book, but I do recommend you also check out other charities' websites to see their privacy statements.

As an added complication, Article 14(3) states that you need to provide the data subject with fair processing information "within a reasonable period after obtaining the personal data, but at the latest within one month." So, if you wish to create a list of new prospects to invite to an event or carry out research into a donor's networks (which I discuss in Section 6.4), you cannot sit on the information you find (any potential new major donors you have identified) until you are ready to contact them. Under GDPR, fair processing requires you to inform them you are holding their data within one month.

But there is an exception to this.

Article 14(5) states that this one month limit shall not apply if "the provision of such information proves impossible or would involve a disproportionate effort…or in so far as the obligation referred to…is likely to render impossible or seriously impair the achievement of the objectives of that processing."

You could argue that when preparing a list of invitees to an event, telling these people that you are processing their data (which could happen months before the event date, to enable you to plan ahead for the event and make it a success) would "seriously impair the achievement of the objectives of that processing", i.e. successfully putting on the event.

I leave it up to you as to whether you think this is a reasonable application of Article 14(5). However, I do feel that if you wish to carry out research into a donor's networks, this exception is unlikely to apply and so you will need to inform those people you identify within a month of when you start processing their data.

3.5 Is the processing lawful?

Article 6 of the GDPR lists six possible conditions to justify the processing of personal data. You must satisfy one of them. If you cannot do so, you're in breach of the law.

Of these six, there are two which are relevant to prospect research: consent and legitimate interests.

3.5.1 Consent

According to Article 4(11), consent is:

> any freely given, specific, informed and unambiguous indication of the data subject's wishes...by a statement or by a clear affirmative action

Just to be clear, Recital 32 adds "Silence, pre-ticked boxes or inactivity should not therefore constitute consent."

The ICO would like consent to be the standard, especially when researching people using external sources of information. But consent raises two clear problems for prospect research.

First, there are situations where we want to research people but do not want to ask for their consent. E.g. Creating a list of invitees to an event or researching a donor's contacts so the donor can invite those contacts to a meeting, an event, a service visit, etc. These are situations in which the person may be put off by the request for consent, even if they would have been perfectly happy to attend an event, or meet up with a canvasser, to learn more about supporting your charity with a major donation.

Second, for a variety of reasons (e.g. they never received the request, they read it but forgot about it), the person may not reply to your written request for consent, even if they don't actually object to you processing their data. But if they don't reply to your request for consent, you cannot research them. Remember, silence or inactivity is not evidence of consent.

And just how would you ask for this consent?

> "We'd like your consent to carry out some research into you to establish if you earn enough money to be able to make a major gift and if you're the sort of person who would like to support our charity."

Awkward, to say the least. And the very opposite of the mutually respectful relationship we wish to develop with our major donors.

These problems can be avoided if we rely on legitimate interests.

3.5.2 Legitimate interests

According to Article 6(1), the processing of personal data is lawful if it is

> necessary for the purposes of the legitimate interests pursued by the controller...except where such interests are overridden by the interests or fundamental rights and freedoms of

Chapter 3 Data protection

the data subject which require protection of personal data.

There are therefore three elements to the legitimate interest condition. The first is to be clear on what the legitimate interests actually are which you are pursuing. The second is the necessity of the data processing. Is it necessary to the legitimate interests of your charity to process the data? The third element is to ensure your processing does not affect the fundamental rights and freedoms of the data subject.

Legitimate interests

Legitimate interest is not a high bar to clear, says Tim Turner:

> Anything that isn't illegal, immoral or secret is likely to be a legitimate interest. Making a profit from a legal business is plainly a legitimate interest, so soliciting a charitable donation or other similarly philanthropic act must also be a legitimate interest.

Clearly, it is a legitimate interest for a charity to raise funds, and if rich people exist who wish to make major donations to charities (which of course they do) then it must be in your charity's legitimate interest to seek major donations from those individuals who may wish to make them to you. Major gift fundraising is clearly a legitimate interest.

Necessity

To use the legitimate interests condition, whatever you do must be necessary. Which it clearly is, as we cannot know who may be interested in our work (if they've not supported us before) or what level of gift to ask for, until we've carried out our research. Research is clearly necessary to major gift fundraising (and major gift fundraising is necessary to your charity to enable it to raise the money it needs to for specific projects – yes?).

The data subject's rights and freedoms

Article 21 states:

> The data subject shall have the right to object, on grounds relating to his or her particular situation, at any time to processing of personal data concerning him or her which is based on point (f) of Article 6(1). [i.e. legitimate interests.]

We *must* be transparent about how we process data so that the data subject is aware of this and is able to object.

If it is in our legitimate interest to carry out prospect research into potential major donors and if it does not affect the rights and freedoms of the donor to do so, then we can do so. This has already been covered in Section 3.3.6, which concluded that prospect research causes no risk to the rights and freedoms of the data subject.

If you are still concerned then, as I said earlier, do what a number of other charities have done and talk to your existing major donors (or your largest or warmest donors), to find out what level of research they regard as reasonable and what level intrusive or harmful. You will then have clear evidence to support your position.

3.6 Is the processing limited to what is adequate, relevant and necessary?

Recital 39 of the GDPR states:

> The personal data should be adequate, relevant and limited to what is necessary for the purposes for which they are processed.

Whenever researching a potential major donor, whether a current supporter or someone new, we need to be mindful of limiting your research to what is relevant and necessary. According to the *Guide to data protection*, "You should not hold more personal data than you need. Nor should the data you hold include irrelevant details."

About ten years ago I attended a fundraising conference at which the head of fundraising for a well-known charity told the audience "I always tell my researchers to find me everything they can about the prospect."

As well as being, in many cases, a colossal waste of time and resources, such a request is highly likely to be in breach of the third data protection principle regarding limiting data processing to what is relevant and necessary.

Producing profiles on prospects and donors which are many pages long with copious amounts of information from numerous different sources cannot help but include information which is irrelevant and unnecessary to the purpose of identifying and cultivating a potential major donor.

But what would count as irrelevant details? For some prospects, it is possible to find out detailed information about their career, their spouse and their children (and all of their careers), as well as their hobbies and interests, and the hobbies and interests of their family. At what point does this information become irrelevant? There is no hard and fast answer, but at the very least you must be able to justify where *you* draw the line, so you can demonstrate that the information you hold on your prospects and donors is relevant and necessary. This is why, when I first research a prospect, I only produce what I term a 'Qualification Profile'. This is a paragraph or two long, or half a page at most, containing nothing more or less than the information required to know whether the prospect is worth cultivating or not. Basic career information, likely gift capacity, inclination to support your charity with a big gift and some due diligence research. *But nothing more.*

For prospects who already support you, you really only need a sentence or two covering their career, their gift capacity and their past support of, and communication with, your charity. Anything more than this I regard as irrelevant and unnecessary – and a potential waste of time until you know whether the prospect wishes to engage with you or not.

3.7 Is the data you hold accurate, up to date and time-limited?

3.7.1 Accurate and up to date

According to Article 5(d) of the GDPR:

> Personal data shall be accurate and, where necessary, kept up to date; every reasonable step must be taken to ensure that personal data that are inaccurate, having regard to the purposes for which they are processed, are erased or rectified without delay

Recital 65 adds:

> The data subject shall have the right to obtain from the controller without undue delay the rectification of inaccurate personal data concerning him or her.

Practically speaking, this means updating data immediately you learn or are told it is inaccurate or out of date, but you must also systematically check your records for inaccurate or outdated information. For example, you should check profiles are accurate and up to date (especially current employment and job title) on an annual basis (any more frequently would be too great a workload, and probably unnecessary, but any less frequently and the information would not be sufficiently up to date). You should also delete profiles that are no longer required (e.g. for donors no longer considered prospects).

In their *Fundraising and regulatory compliance* guidelines, the ICO states that keeping records up to date does not mean you have a mandate to seek out a donor's new address when they move house:

> If you find that an individual has moved house, you should update your records to reflect that. This will be enough to comply with Principle 4; you don't need to seek out their new address.

In other words, it is enough to mark the donor's address as appropriate, e.g. gone away, moved, address not valid, etc.

However, the ICO is only giving their *interpretation* of the DPA. As long as you are mindful of not being intrusive or harmful towards your donors, I believe you are justified in looking for new addresses for *current* donors. In practice, this means using only obviously publicly available sources for your information, i.e. the electoral roll or phone book. But having said that, if you have the donor's email address or phone number, you should use those channels of communication to ask the donor's permission to update their address details.

3.7.2 Time-limited

Article 5(e) of the GDPR states:

Chapter 3 Data protection

> Personal data shall be kept in a form which permits identification of data subjects for no longer than is necessary for the purposes for which the personal data are processed.

This principle is closely related to the third and fourth principles. As the ICO says:

> Ensuring personal data is disposed of when no longer needed will reduce the risk that it will become inaccurate, out of date or irrelevant.

You need to be mindful of your charity's overall procedure for archiving or deleting older records, but also be aware of the special circumstances that relate to major gift fundraising. For example, potential major donors who have been added to your database but then never invited to an event should be removed from the database promptly, if you do not plan to invite them to any other events.

And it is not just data held on the database, but also data in documents and spreadsheets – in electronic and print form – that must be deleted or destroyed when no longer needed.

Is it enough to archive old data or must it be deleted?

The ICO recognises there are some situations in which archiving old data is appropriate, but in the *Guide to data protection* they also state:

> ...there is a significant difference between permanently deleting a record and archiving it. If a record is archived or stored offline, this should

reduce its availability and the risk of misuse or mistake. However, you should only archive a record (rather than delete it) if you still need to hold it. You must be prepared to give subject access to it, and to comply with the data protection principles.

In practice, records that are no longer needed – especially when the subject has made no donation – should be deleted rather than archived.

3.8 Is the processing safe and secure?

Article 32 of the GDPR advises that you must "implement appropriate technical and organisational measures to ensure a level of security appropriate to the risk." Specifically,

> In assessing the appropriate level of security account shall be taken in particular of the risks that are presented by processing, in particular from accidental or unlawful destruction, loss, alteration, unauthorised disclosure of, or access to personal data transmitted, stored or otherwise processed.

I presume that your charity already has a high degree of security when processing data: passwords to protect computers, your database and even individual documents; paper files kept in locked drawers or filing cabinets; appropriate security measures to stop any old person from wandering into your office and looking at what they want, etc.

Chapter 3 Data protection

But when carrying out research into people, you must be particularly careful to avoid the following (each of which I have known people to do in my time):

- Leaving printed copies of profiles lying around on your desk where anyone can see them (or take them, should they choose)
- Emailing or posting profiles to people who do not work for your charity (e.g. other major donors or other guests to an event)
- Taking profiles of event invitees to that event and then leaving the document lying around for anyone to see
- Putting profiles, documents or spreadsheets of donors' data on a memory stick without encrypting it (if you are working away from your office, for example)
- Throwing away printed copies of profiles in the recycling bin – they should be securely shredded.

3.9 Next steps

The whole rationale for writing this chapter can be summed up in the following quote by Tim Turner:

> If you can make a solid case that what you're doing complies by referring to what the DPA / GDPR says, ICO staff may be reluctant to substitute their judgment for yours in the event of complaint.

If you are carrying out prospect research, you need to make that case. This chapter will help, I hope, but you should also do the following:

1. Read the ICO's *Guide to Data Protection*. And look out for any other guides they produce concerning the GDPR or the Data Protection Act 2018.
2. Read the GDPR so that you are thoroughly familiar with it (I would read the Articles first, specifically 1 to 34, and then Recitals 1 to 88). Print a copy out and go through it with a highlighter, marking those parts particularly pertinent to major gift fundraising.
3. Read Tim Turner's guide to fundraising and data protection. It is not perfect – he is not a fundraiser, as he admits – but it is not far off. And it contains a very useful section on the Privacy and Electronic Communications Regulations, which sit alongside the GDPR and give people specific privacy rights in relation to electronic communications.
4. Talk to your existing major donors to find out what level of research they regard as reasonable and what level intrusive or harmful.
5. Talk to your colleagues in other charities to see what they are doing. But don't just assume what they are doing is right, or right for *you*.

In the end this chapter is just my own views, thoughts and feelings and *not* legal advice. It is up to *you* to ensure you are complying with data protection legislation but comply with it you must.

Data Protection Resources

GDPR (linking Articles with the relevant Recitals):
http://www.privacy-regulation.eu/en/index.htm

ICO's Guide to Data Protection:
https://ico.org.uk/for-organisations/guide-to-data-protection/

ICO's Guide to the Privacy and Electronic Comms Regulations:
https://ico.org.uk/for-organisations/guide-to-pecr/

Fundraising And Data Protection, A survival guide for the uninitiated by Tim Turner:
http://2040training.co.uk/wp-content/uploads/2017/03/Fundraising-DP-guide.pdf

4

That thing you do

Before we finally get down to the nitty gritty of identifying prospects, it is vital that you answer this fundamental question: do you know all the services which your charity offers? More specifically, can you answer the following three questions?

1. What services does your organisation offer?
2. How are they offered?
3. Where are they offered?

As we saw in the last chapter, one powerful motivational factor is the extent to which a donor's gift really makes a difference to your charity's work. By answering these three questions you will be able to identify those areas of your work, those specific projects, which will especially demonstrate to potential donors the impact their donation will have on your work, making a donation to your charity a more attractive proposition than a donation to another charity.

Chapter 4 That thing you do

This is one of the reasons why one-off capital campaigns are so successful at raising money from major donors. It is easy to demonstrate the impact a major gift will have with a new building or refurbishment and there will be an added incentive for the donor if you follow common practice and offer to name a room, a floor, or the whole building (for a large enough donation), after the donor. If you are not launching a capital campaign of this sort, but wish to attract major donors to support ongoing work, then the most obvious way to demonstrate the impact their donation will have is to identify specific projects whose cost equates with the level of donation you are seeking (or a project which can be easily broken down into chunks whose cost equates with the donation you are seeking). You need to be able to demonstrate to the donor that their gift paid for the research fellowship that made a certain piece of work possible, or paid for a new sewerage system to be built in a developing country or paid for the training and annual costs of one of the people who operates your helpline, providing vital support to those in need. As you see, I am using the term project quite loosely here. It must be some tangible thing which will attract the support of your major donors.

Another key motivational factor is caring for your cause and so if you can identify projects which you believe will really appeal to the prospect in this regard you will have a far greater chance of engaging their interest and prompting them to support your charity with a major gift. Having a thorough knowledge of the services your charity offers will allow you to do this.

Supporting local causes is another significant motivational factor for major donors, so it is in your best interest to identify all those areas around the country where you provide a service, so as to be able to attract prospects from that area.

To be really sure of creating a comprehensive list of your services, I suggest you break down the three questions listed above into more discrete parts.

1. What services does your organisation offer?
- Specialist advice (technical, medical, legal, local)
- Support (emotional, financial)
- Care (of people, animals, buildings, artefacts)
- Training (for carers, volunteers, specialist work)
- Funding (research, volunteer groups)
- Research (into the causes and prevention/treatment of a particular problem)
- Campaigning (the public, the government, the EU, specialist bodies or associations)
- Education (of the public, carers, specialist staff)

2. How are these services offered?
- Verbally (telephone, conferences, training, one to one meetings, radio/TV adverts)
- Written (appeal mailings, email, newsletter, annual report, website, poster, newspaper adverts)

Chapter 4 That thing you do

- Nature of personnel (volunteers, paid staff, trained specialists, regional branches, affiliated clubs)
- Directly by your organisation and/or through another organisation (hospital, university, regional branch or club)

3. Where are these services offered?

- Geography (nationally or locally? Specific geographical areas of focus or UK wide?)
- Structure (one main office or many regional offices?)
- Venue (via a hospital, university, school, cathedral, museum, local centres)

Clearly there is some crossover between each section, but the idea is to produce a *comprehensive* list of your services and not (at least, to begin with) a neat and tidy list. You can tidy it up once you've considered every aspect of your organisation's services.

To be really sure that you have covered all possibilities, do ask other people in your organisation to contribute: volunteers, admin staff and, above all, the service providers themselves. You want to get as comprehensive a list as you can to ensure you can identify the best projects to present to prospects.

That is the first step. The second step is to put a clear, discrete monetary value to as many of your projects and services as you can to create what is called a wish list. This is a list of items, ranging in cost from the minimum donation size that you count as a major gift up to, well, whatever you want, which will allow you to offer each of your prospects a project or service ideally suited to their interests and donation potential. Valuing projects and services in this way is naturally easier for some than others and you may sometimes need to be a little creative in how you present the information, but it is vitally important that you do not simply ask your prospect for £10,000 "to support our vital work" but rather you ask them for £10,000 "as this is the annual cost of equipment and research materials used by one of our research scientists".

5
Digging into your database

5.1 Past major donors

If you want to identify major gift prospects, the most obvious place to start looking is your fundraising database. Current donors are far more likely than non-donors to satisfy the motivational factors of passion for the cause, affinity with your charity and a belief that your charity is worthy. They may also have a person-to-person connection with your charity and, through their knowledge of your work, appreciate the impact a major gift would have on your charity, so they really are the ideal group in which to start looking for prospects.

Unless you already have a very good idea of the history of giving to your charity, then I strongly recommend, before anything else, searching your database for all previous major donors. Not only will this give you an idea of the level of previous philanthropic support for your charity (always useful to know before launching a fundraising appeal), it may also throw up a number of prospects; if someone has given you a significant donation before, they may be prepared to do so again. If you are not confident in searching your database using queries or reports, do ask someone in your IT or database team to help you. It is important that you find the right information and do not miss anything.

As they say with financial investment, past performance is no guarantee of future performance, but even so, knowing that a prospect has given you £20,000 in the past is a very good guide to their being able to do so again. You do get one-off donations, especially to capital appeals, but unless you know that someone's circumstances have changed, knowing what they gave you in the past is one of the best indicators of what they can give now.

At what level should your search for past donors start? That is really up to you, as charities differ widely in the level of philanthropic support they have received in the past. If you really have no idea, then start by searching for donors of £500 or more and if this results in a list of more than 100 people, raise the amount to £1,000 and try again. If, on the other hand, you get no results, then lower the amount to £100, say, and try again. If your search brings up little or nothing, then do not get disheartened – this is what this book is for; to find people who *will* support your charity with a major gift.

How far back should your search go? As far back as your database goes, certainly, and even further if you have the time and inclination to search through filing

Chapter 5 Digging into your database

cabinets of old correspondence (which may not be on your database), your charity archives and accounts. When I worked at Great Ormond Street Hospital Children's Charity, I decided to compile a list of all significant donors to the hospital from its foundation in 1852 to the present day. By significant, I was looking for anyone who was well known or notable in some way: celebrities, politicians, that sort of thing. Obviously, there were no databases in the 'good old days' of Charles Dickens (who was one of the hospital's first significant donors) and so a considerable amount of old-fashioned research was required; I could not simply turn on a computer and search the internet.

I read books and articles on the history of the hospital, waded through newspaper cuttings and other archive material in the hospital museum, and sifted through reams of faded computer printouts kept by the Finance Department from the days of the Hospital's Wishing Well Appeal of the 1980s. Some very interesting names came up, including several forebears of contemporary wealthy individuals.

For many charities, such extensive archived material is not available, but unless you look for it, you won't know what useful information *is* to be found in past charity annual reports, supporters' newsletters and charity magazines – or who you may uncover.

One-off donations above a certain level are only one sign of wealth. Another sign is a series of donations, spread over a year, or two years, or five years, that add up to a significant amount. If a donor has given donations of between £50 and £100 every few months for several years, the first search of donations of £500 or more will not pick them up. Nevertheless, their donations may add up to several thousand pounds over the years, indicating they may be wealthy and worth marking as a prospect, so do carry out a search for people whose total donations per year or over a larger period, adds up to £1,000 or more.

5.2 Private banks

Identifying current donors who use a private bank account is possibly the best technique to identify prospects in your database. Private Banks offer specialist services (wealth management, tax advice, loans for yachts) for those with a significant level of wealth and as such, they generally require their clients to have, at least, several hundred thousand pounds with which to open an account. There is no guarantee that someone with a private bank account *is* wealthy, but it is much more likely than not.

If you look at the table on pages 66-67 you will see the level of investible assets generally required to open an account with a private bank. Investible assets are those that can be readily invested, which excludes property, art, land and other fixed assets which may figure in a person's 'total wealth' but which cannot be invested (and are mostly irrelevant to their ability to make a major donation). The figures given are based

Chapter 5 Digging into your database

on the bank's own website, news articles and interviews, and banking and finance websites. They are not meant to be representative of *everyone* who has an account with one of these banks but just to represent the assets or salary typically required to open an account. Coutts, for example, upped the level of investible assets required from £500k to £1m in 2011, but I have kept the £500k figure as many of their pre-2011 clients must still have between £500k and £1m in investible assets.

There are two ways to identify prospects with a private bank account. The first is to look out for donations received through a private bank cheque. Ask your post room, your Finance department, or whoever it is that banks the cheques, to look out for any cheques that are not from one of the high street banks. If you use a fulfilment house to handle your big appeals, then do check if they are able to do this. It is not hard; cheques from private banks often have quite distinctive designs and are easy to spot.

The second way is to search for private bank accounts already listed in your database. The easiest way to do this is to export the whole list of bank names (with the name of the account holder) into a password protected spreadsheet, sort them alphabetically, and delete the high street banks from the list. You do not need individual bank account details for this search and so *do not* export those.

Prospect Research

Bank	Investible Assets (or salary)
Adam & Co	£100k
Arbuthnot Latham	£500k
Bank of Scotland Private Banking	£250k (£100k salary)
Banque Havilland	£1m
Barclays Wealth	£500k
BNP Paribas Wealth Management	£1m
Brown Shipley	£500k
Butterfield Bank	£1m
C Hoare & Co	£1m
Cater Allen Private Bank	£100k
Child & Co (RBS)	£100k
Citi Private Bank	£5m
Coutts & Co	£500k
Credit Suisse	£1m
Deutsche Bank	£250k
Drummonds Bank	£100k
Duncan Lawrie Private Banking	£500k
HSBC Private Bank	£3m
JP Morgan Private Bank	£3m
Julius Bär	£2m
Kleinwort Benson	£500k
Lloyds Private Banking	£250k (£100k salary)
Lombard Odier	£5m
Morgan Stanley Private Bank	£2.5m
Natwest Private Banking	£100k (£100k salary)
Nedbank Private Wealth	£275k (£80k salary)

Chapter 5 Digging into your database

Pictet	£5m
Rathbone Brothers	£100k
Rothschild	£100k
Royal Bank of Canada	£500k
RBS Private Banking	£100k
SG Private Banking Hambros	£1m
Standard Chartered	£1m
UBS	£500k
Union Bancaire Privée	£500k
Weatherbys Bank	£300k salary

Some databases do not display bank names, but only sort codes. This requires a slight variation on the search above. Export the entire list of sort codes and then, working on the principle that rarity equals private bank, check those sort codes that appear the least. You can use an online sort code identifier (found by searching Google or Bing) to determine if the sort code corresponds to a private bank.

5.3 Occupation

The next technique to identify prospects on your database is to search by occupation or job title. Knowing someone's profession and seniority can tell you a great deal about their wealth (and their likely networks, which can be very useful as we will see in Section 6.4).

Anyone with a senior job title such as Chief Executive, Chairman, Chief Operating Office, Chief Finance Director, Managing Director, Partner,

Managing Partner, President, Vice President or Founder, is worth flagging up as a prospect.

There are also various finance-related job titles that are worth looking for. E.g. Fund Manager, Hedge Fund Manager, Banker, Investment Banker, Merchant Banker, Private Banker, Investment Analyst, Equity Analyst, Equity Trader, Financier, Financial Broker, Stockbroker, Broker, Investment Manager, and any variations on those titles.

The finance sector does not have the monopoly on wealth, so you should also look for the following: Solicitor, Barrister, Diplomat, QC, Broker, Trader, Oil Trader, Oil Broker, Shipbroker, Investor, Venture Capitalist, Racehorse Trainer, actor, footballer – indeed, anything you can think of that may yield a suitable result.

Your best option may be to export the relevant details (name and occupation or job title) from your whole database into a spreadsheet and then sort the job titles alphabetically. Then you can go through them one by one, keeping the most promising ones and deleting the rest. This will also make sure you pick up (and correct!) any misspelled job titles – Fund Manger, Stckbroker, Barister – which inevitably creep into every database.

A related search is to look for directors of your current or past corporate supporters. Many senior staff get personally involved with the charities which they are currently supporting (organising fundraising events or volunteering) and so you should talk to your

Chapter 5 Digging into your database

Corporate department to find out who the most likely prospects are from this group.

5.4 Email addresses

You can also identify someone's profession through their work email address.

As with the job title search, the best method to follow is to export the details of everyone on your database with an email address into a spreadsheet. I then sort them alphabetically by domain name and go through the list one by one to identify those who may be wealthy (e.g. legal and accountancy firms, wealth management and other finance companies and also local businesses). If you are unsure about a domain name, simply copy and paste it into your web browser to see what the company is. (To sort the list of email addresses alphabetically by domain name, perform a 'find and replace' action on the list using Ctrl F, putting *@ in the **Find what** field and a blank space in the **Replace with** field. This will remove the prospect's name and the @ sign from the list of emails, leaving only the domain names which can then be sorted alphabetically). Do be aware that certain companies do not use their full name in an email address (e.g. Goldman Sachs use @gs.com and Morgan Stanley use @ms.com).

It can take some time to sort through a list of email addresses, just as it can do to sort through job titles, but once you have deleted all the Yahoo, BT, Gmail and other generic email addresses, you should soon begin to see some potential prospects. If you really do find yourself having to look through tens of thousands of email addresses, then you may find it easier to search for specific company email addresses (banks and other financial companies, accountancy firms and law firms, most obviously).

5.5 Property

The next technique uses property value to identify wealthy prospects.

An expensive property is no guarantee of wealth. If someone has lived in the same home for 20 or 30 years, the value of the property could have shot up since it was bought, even though the owner may actually have little disposable income. (But if you should find someone like this, do not ignore them; they may wish to leave you a residuary legacy).

Nor can you tell from a property website whether a person is mortgaged up to the eyeballs or not, but given that a mortgage is a product of their salary, the value of their property can give you some idea of their wealth. A mortgage provider will not knowingly give a large mortgage to someone unless they earn (or are expected to earn) a large salary to pay for it. It is a reasonable premise that someone in a £5m property is more likely to be capable of making a significant gift than someone in a £100,000 property

Chapter 5 Digging into your database

5.5.1 Postcodes

One simple way to identify expensive properties on your database is to search for them by postcode. This is especially worthwhile if you are a local charity and the majority of your donors come from the local community. You can readily identify prospects who live in the most expensive streets in your area using Mouseprice or Zoopla, which both list the most expensive streets by postcode in towns throughout the UK.

I prefer to do this using Mouseprice. To find local postcodes with the most expensive properties, simply go to their website and select the 'Area Guide' tab at the top of the screen. Enter the postcode prefix for your particular area (e.g. RG4) and then select 'Most expensive' from the list of street rankings for that area. When the list of 30 postcodes appears, click on each street in turn to find the exact postcode. Then search for anyone in your database who lives at that postcode.

A variation of this search is to list the postcodes of your past major donors and search for other donors on your database who have the same postcode. The premise here is that those donors who live in the same (presumably expensive) area as your existing major donors may also be wealthy.

5.5.2 House Names

Another way to identify expensive property owners, albeit a more time-consuming one, is to run a query which searches your database (i.e. the first line of their address) for those names which are indicative of a large country house: Abbey, Castle, Court, Hall, House, Manor or Park. But be careful; this search can bring up a very large number of unwanted addresses (Manor Road, Castle Street, Park Hill, etc.), unless you specifically filter them out in your query. You can reduce the number further by selecting only those who have given a donation in the last year, or within the last few years.

If you find you cannot filter out these unwanted street names, import the whole list into a spreadsheet and sort the list A to Z. This will bring all the addresses with a number to the top of the list – 1 Manor Road, 2 Park Hill, 3 Castle Street – so that you can easily delete them, leaving only the house names you want.

Then you will need to check the value of the houses in your list using a property website such as Zoopla or Mouseprice to identify the expensive properties.

5.6 Titles

Searching for titled donors is another simple technique to identify wealthy prospects or those with good networks; both hereditary titles (Duke, Duchess, Marquess, Marchioness, Earl, Countess, Viscount, Viscountess) and also those conferred upon the recipient (Dame, Lady, Baroness, Lord and Sir).

Having a hereditary title is little or no guarantee of wealth, although some hereditary peerages do come with an impressive amount of land and other assets. But the phrase "asset-rich, cash-poor" exists for a reason and so do not be fooled into thinking that a large mansion and huge estate means the person is a good prospect for a major donation. The same is true of those who are awarded life peerages, knighthoods or damehoods, but there is a significant difference between the two. Unlike those who have gained their title through birth, these people will have excelled in some way in their particular sphere of life, which has culminated in the award of a peerage, knighthood or damehood. They will have certain experiences, skills and connections which make them ideal as prospects – if they cannot make a major donation themselves they may be able to introduce you to others who can.

5.7 Wealth screening

Wealth screening companies such as Factary and Prospecting for Gold compare your database with their own database of wealthy people (generally those with a net worth of £1m or more). They use a wide variety of publicly available sources (company and trust annual reports, rich lists, shareholder databases, national and regional newspapers, company websites and property data) to ensure that their data is as comprehensive and accurate as possible.

Subject to your individual circumstances, they will carry out an exploratory search for free, so that you know how many of your prospects are on their database. Do be sure you are transparent with your donors about screening your database, or you will fall foul of data protection legislation. Check with the screening company itself if you are unsure.

A screening can be very useful, but do not think of it as something to be done *instead* of the other identification techniques described above. The two are complimentary. If you do have prospects who are worth £1m or more, a screening is likely to find many of them (as will some of the other techniques), but if you have prospects who fall below that level, but may still be worth cultivating for a significant gift – I'm thinking here of doctors, accountants, solicitors and other professionals – then you will need to use the other techniques to identify them.

5.8 DIY wealth screening

If the cost of getting your data screened is beyond your budget, or you have too small a database to warrant a screening, then you might want to consider the DIY option. This involves going through the Sunday Times Rich List, or a local rich list, person by person and searching for them on your database to see if they have ever given you a donation.

It almost goes without saying that this is very time consuming, but you can ease the pain, so to speak, by doing just a little searching each day, or each week, depending upon your other duties. Most people can find half an hour each day, or every other day, to feed names into their database. And you will find that discovering that first millionaire more than makes up for the hours spent entering names without a result.

The confidence with which you can be sure that the person you have found on your database is the person listed in the rich list very much depends upon the person's name. How many people will there be on your database called Hamish Ogston, Thor Bjorgolfsson or Kirsten Rausing? If one of these comes up, it's a pretty safe bet they're the one and only. But as far as a name like John Smith is concerned, your best option is to check the home address on your database against known addresses for the Rich List John Smith, to see if they match. We will look at how to find someone's home, work or charitable trust address in chapter 6.

5.9 Conclusion

You may have thought, when going through this chapter, "Oh, that search won't apply to my charity." Whilst there is no doubt that some of these searches will bring up more results for larger, national charities than smaller, local charities, they are still worth doing; you never know what golden nugget may be buried in the ground until you take a look.

And I am well aware that several of these searches – those involving job title, email, house names and postcodes in particular – can be time consuming, but you are looking for people who can make a *major* gift to your charity, so it is very much worth your while spending some time looking for them. Even half an hour a day will soon add up to a substantial amount of time over a period of several weeks. Just remember to always be methodical and keep everything in nice manageable chunks. It is for this reason that I recommend importing each search you do into a separate page of a spreadsheet; it helps to keep your work neat and tidy and it is very easy to evaluate your progress and demonstrate it to your head of department, trustees, or other senior personnel, as necessary.

Chapter 5 Digging into your database

Websites

Registers of Scotland:
www.ros.gov.uk/services/ownership-search

Zoopla: www.zoopla.co.uk

Mouseprice: www.mouseprice.com

Prospecting for Gold:
http://prospectingforgold.co.uk

Million Pound Property Database:
http://prospectingforgold.co.uk/wealth/#MPP

Factary: www.factary.com

The Sunday Times Rich List:
www.thesundaytimes.co.uk/sto/public/richlist

6

Widening the search

6.1 Competitor analysis

According to Theresa Lloyd, "Donors who care deeply about a generic cause, whether child poverty or opera, may well support more than one charity or institution addressing those issues."

With this in mind, an obvious place to look for new major gift prospects is to charities with a similar cause to your own. This can be particularly helpful if you do not (yet) have a supporter database of your own or it is only small.

It may strike you as a little unethical to try to poach another charity's donors, but you shouldn't feel bad about it. In the first place, as Lloyd states, many donors are happy to support more than one charity which concerns itself with their favourite cause. Do not think that you will be taking away money from another charity just because you attract the attention of one of their major donors. If your charity is worthy of support, there is no reason why the donor will not decide to support both charities.

Chapter 6 Widening the search

Secondly, charities that deal with similar causes can have quite different projects or areas of specialisation. There are many charities that help underprivileged children, for example, but they often have very different areas of specialisation: some work locally, some nationally and some internationally; some offer children once-in-a-lifetime holidays or grant wishes to allow long-held dreams to be fulfilled; some provide clothing or other essentials in winter; some aim to protect those who are at risk of physical or emotional harm; some try to identify the causes of under privilege and seek to change them; and so on.

Finally, and perhaps most pragmatically, don't think that other charities won't try to poach *your* major donors! It's a competitive marketplace out there and although charities may not compete with the same cut-throat vigour as other organisations, there is competition for donors. If you really believe that your charity is worthy of a donor's support, then you owe it to that donor to make yourself known to them, even if they already support similar charities or causes.

Many charities list their significant individual, trust and company donors in their annual report and also list them on their website. Finding them involves a two-step process. Step 1 is to create a list of those charities with a similar cause to yours. Step 2 is to check their annual report and their website. Annual reports are invariably available to download from the organisation's website but for English and Welsh charities you can also download them from the Charity

Prospect Research

Commission's Register of Charities website. The Register of Charities contains details of registered charities in England and Wales with an income of over £5,000 a year. (The Office of the Scottish Charity Regulator performs a similar function for charities based in Scotland, but it does not allow you to download annual reports).

If you are not sure which organisations have similar causes to your own, you can find out by doing an advanced search on the Register of Charities website (England and Wales only) or the website Charity Choice (which provides information on every single charity registered in England and Wales and a large number from Scotland). To find charities with a similar cause to your own on the Register of Charities website you need to use the Filter menu down the left hand side of the page; specifically, the filter options **What the Charity does**, **Who the charity helps** and **How the charity operates**. If your search brings up too many charities, you can use the income filter to de-select the smaller charities.

To search on Charity Choice, select **Find a Charity** from their homepage menu to bring up a list of charity sectors. Select the sector that most closely represents your charity and then select the appropriate sub-category to bring up the relevant charities. Unlike the Register of Charities search facility, you cannot exclude charities by income and so you will have to check each of the charities in the list one by one to see whether they list major donors.

Chapter 6 Widening the search

6.2 Who's Who

Who's Who contains autobiographies of some 33,000 "noteworthy and influential" people in the UK and abroad. The online version is available without subscription through library membership. You can find your local library and the research resources they provide here: **www.gov.uk/local-library-services**. If you are after a particular resource, your local library should be able to advise you as to the nearest library which offers that resource.

Although being listed in *Who's Who* is not a sign of wealth, it is a sign that your prospect has been successful in some sphere of life and this success may have brought financial gain with it. You will have to use your own judgement, based on the career information listed in their biography, to determine whether you consider them to be a likely prospect or not. Each entrant provides the details for their autobiography, which means you can be sure of the accuracy of the information (which is independently checked). What varies is the amount of information supplied by each entrant; some are happy to provide a detailed autobiography, others may only supply a line or two and no contact information (but such brief autobiographies are rare).

The ease with which you can find prospects in *Who's Who* will depend upon the sort of charity you are. We saw in chapter 2 that location is a powerful motivating factor for major gift prospects. If you wish to identify prospects in a certain location, you can simply type the relevant town or city into the search field at the top of the screen and then select the Address tab to list those people who list that town/city in their address. Then it is just a matter of going through the people in the list one by one, noting the likely prospects for further research later on.

If you want to search for prospects across the UK who will support a certain cause (i.e. the one related to your charity), your task becomes more difficult. Most entrants to *Who's Who* list their interests in the Recreations field (football, opera, the environment, dogs, cats, stamp collecting, etc.) and so if there is an interest which matches up with your cause, then you may find a variety of prospects. As before, type the relevant word to identify your cause or charity into the search field at the top of the screen and then select the Recreations tab to list those people who mention the word in their Recreations.

This search is easier for some causes than others. People will readily list environmental concerns, animals, family, sports and even fundraising events amongst their recreations, but no one puts 'Helping HIV positive prostitutes' or 'supporting urinary incontinence'. For this reason, you may have more success looking at their Career. The search process is just the same: type the relevant word to identify your cause or charity into the search field at the top of the screen and then select the Career tab to list those people who mention the word in their career. The idea

Chapter 6 Widening the search

behind this search it to bring up trustees of charities, volunteers and other organisations related to your charity, but it can be somewhat hit and miss.

Who's Who also has an advanced search facility, which you may find beneficial. Just select **More search options** under the search field to open it.

6.3 Local people

Who's Who is not the only sources of local prospects. As a general rule, newspapers do not run stories about people unless there is something 'newsworthy' about them and one of those things is money. For this reason, looking for national or local newspaper articles for people who are connected to a particular location can be a very good way to uncover prospects.

You can search many newspapers online simply by using Google or Bing, but these search engines do not capture everything and so for local newspapers it is worthwhile searching the newspaper's own website (you can find your local newspapers by simply searching online for "local newspapers" and your specific area).

To maximise your chances of success, imagine how the news article might be phrased and phrase your search string accordingly or check out the latest copy of your local paper for any articles about local businessmen and women and see what phrases they use to describe them.

Prospect Research

As an example, to find local businessmen and women in my home town of Reading, I would try the following searches:

> "local businessman" "Reading"
> "local businesswoman" "Reading"
> "born in Reading"
> "grew up in Reading"
> "lived/lives in/near Reading"
> "born in Reading" "businessman"
> "born in Reading" "businesswoman"
> "local tycoon" "Reading"
> "Reading-born tycoon/businessman/woman"
> "Reading-born philanthropist"
> "local philanthropist" "Reading"

This is where local knowledge can be very useful. Try to find someone – a Rotarian or someone who has worked in the area for years – who knows the local businesses; they may be able to provide some invaluable leads. Your local Chamber of Commerce can also be a good source of local knowledge. Go to the British Chambers of Commerce homepage and select your appropriate region from the drop down list on the top right-hand side of the screen, under **Find your local chamber**. This will bring up the region's contact details and website. Then follow the link to their website. The amount of information which each local chamber provides on their site does vary, but at the very least they should provide details of their CEO or Chamber board members, including contact details.

Chapter 6 Widening the search

Some provide much more information, including details of their members (a useful source of prospects) and networking events (another useful source of prospects, if you are allowed to attend).

6.4 Trustees & donors' networks

As we saw in chapter 2, being asked to make a donation by a friend or someone you respect can be a powerful motivating force. You can use this to your advantage by asking your trustees and senior staff, and those major donors with whom you are particularly close, to introduce their wealthy friends and business colleagues to your charity.

Some trustees and donors may be happy to help you in this way, others will simply refuse, and the rest will fall somewhere between the two and need some gentle persuasion before they are willing to give you the names of their friends and colleagues. For this reason, before you approach a trustee or major donor for their help you should carry out some research into their networks, to find out who they know who may be capable of a major gift. This will help to counter the common objections that they "really don't know anyone", that a particular contact "doesn't have any money" or "won't want to support us." You will be more likely to overcome such objections if you can show evidence of their contacts' wealth or philanthropy.

Prospect Research

Researching a trustee or donor's networks before you approach them will also mean that you are not totally reliant upon their opinion (or memory) as to who would be the best person to approach; don't assume they will know or remember who amongst their friends is worth approaching and who isn't.

Be warned; some contacts are very difficult to uncover (friendships made through a private club or dinner party) but work colleagues, fellow charitable trustees, former school and university friends, are easier to find.

The most obvious place to start looking for a prospect's friends and work colleagues is your fundraising database. Many databases allow you to link donors who are known to each other through a Relationships or Connections feature, but contacts may also be listed under general Notes or, indeed, some other section of your database. You know your database better than I do, so consider each of the different ways in which contacts may be recorded on it and check them all for each prospect whose networks you are researching.

If your prospect is a company director then check Companies House for the other directors of each company (check their start and end dates, so you know who overlapped with your prospect and by how much). Then check your database to see if any of these other directors already support you.

Another easy check is to look in the Register of Charities for the other trustees of any foundations or

Chapter 6 Widening the search

charities on which the prospect sits. The Register only lists current or recent trustees (in their most recent annual reports). To discover older relationships, you will need to look at the prospect's profile in *Who's Who*. These two are also the resources to check for old school and university friends. Once you know which school or university your prospect went to, you can easily identify others who went to the same school or university by searching the education section of *Who's Who*. Bear in mind that certain alumni are far more likely to know or remember each other than other alumni. For example, those of a similar age, those who studied the same degree at university or went to the same Oxbridge college, and those who have an interest or sport in common.

It is important to realise that just because two people are directors of the same company, trustees of the same charity, or went to the same school or university, it does not automatically follow that they know each other. This is especially the case for universities, larger companies and charities. But if the charitable foundation is the prospect's own vehicle for giving away their money, or it is a family vehicle, then the trustee is highly likely to know the other trustees very well. And even if two people do know each other, it does not automatically follow that they *like* each other. So, when you show your finished list of friends and business colleagues to the prospect, do not be surprised if the prospect either does not know, or does not wish to approach, some or even many of the names on your list. That is just the luck of the draw. As it is the trustee (or major donor) who will be making the introductions, or sending the invitations (if you are organising an event), you must be led by them. If they are not comfortable approaching a particular person, then you must accept that, otherwise the whole exercise can become completely counter-productive; worse than if you had tried to approach the prospect's friends and colleagues on your own.

And finally, do not forget your obligation from May 2018 under the GDPR to inform those people you are researching within one month of when you first process their data (assuming you have not done so before, if they are already a donor, for example).

6.5 Conclusion

You should now be in possession of several lists of prospects; perhaps as many as 10 or more lists if you have been able to carry out all of the techniques I've described in the last two chapters. Although these techniques are designed to select wealthy prospects who either already support your charity, or who are more likely to want to do so than most people, they are not fool-proof. Some of them are based on some rather broad assumptions and so to prevent you wasting your time by trying to solicit a major gift from someone who cannot make one, or who is very unlikely to want to support your charity with a major gift, you need to go through your prospects one by one and

Chapter 6 Widening the search

qualify them. Qualification is the process by which you determine whether the prospects you have tentatively identified actually have the ability and inclination to support you with a major gift. If you decide upon closer inspection that a prospect is either incapable of making a major gift or unlikely to give one to your charity, then they must be discarded. The remaining qualified prospects should then be ranked by the largest single donation they can make (their *gift capacity*) and by how likely they are to want to support you with a major gift (their *inclination*).

Websites

Register of Charities:
http://beta.charitycommission.gov.uk/charity-search

Charity Choice: www.charitychoice.co.uk

Who's Who: www.ukwhoswho.com

Local Library Services: www.gov.uk/local-library-services

Local Giving: https://localgiving.com

British Chambers of Commerce:
www.britishchambers.org.uk

192.com: www.192.com

7

Qualification

7.1 Qualification as triage

The process of qualification is not about in-depth research. Rather, it is about being able, as quickly and easily as you can, to decide whether a prospect is likely to be willing and able to make a major gift and if they are, how willing and at what level of gift. A useful analogy is that of triage in hospitals. In the process of triage, the hospital is not concerned with treating or curing the patient there and then, but with ascertaining the extent of the person's injuries and the best course of action to take. It is about making quick, accurate, effective decisions. Qualification should be the same. You do not want to spend hours delving into your prospect's career; you just want to be able to make as quick a decision as you can then move on to the next person. Above all, at this early stage you want to avoid spending hours creating a detailed profile for each prospect. Why? The following is a typical fundraising scenario in many charities up and down the country:

Prospect Research

1. A senior figure (head of the fundraising department, chief executive or trustee) identifies a prospect (perhaps they met them at a dinner, or saw them on the database or just looked in the Sunday Times Rich List).

2. They email the person responsible for prospect research and ask them to create a 'full profile' of the prospect.

3. The researcher (who may be too junior to object or simply does not know any better) then spends between several hours and the whole day creating the profile (for this is how long it can take to completely research somebody from scratch). It may run to many pages.

4. The researcher emails the profile to the senior figure, who then spends an hour or two reading it and attempting to memorise the more pertinent points. A process which is hampered by these points being dispersed throughout the multi-page document.

5. The senior figure then contacts the prospect …who it turns out is not in the least bit interested in making a major gift.

This is, as I'm sure you can appreciate, a colossal waste of time. Unfortunately, in many charities it has become the norm to request a full profile for each new prospect found. Some may even view it as best practice – but it is not; especially if the prospect has never supported your charity before. And such charities are very probably falling foul of data protection legislation which requires that the data you process be relevant

Chapter 7 Qualification

and limited to what is necessary. What the researcher should have been asked to produce is a qualification profile (as discussed in Chapter 3, section 3.5) Just a paragraph or two long, or half a page at most, containing nothing more or less than the information required to know whether the prospect is worth cultivating or not. Why waste time on more detailed research until you know whether the prospect wishes to engage with you?

To qualify prospects effectively you will need to become familiar with a variety of web-based research resources. What I suggest you do, as I take you through the resources you will need, is create a folder in your web browser called Research Resources and bookmark in this folder all of the resources I discuss (the relevant URLs are listed at the end of the chapter), so you have them readily to hand when you need them. And I do urge you to join a library. Library membership can provide you with free access to a wide variety of online resources.

7.2 Google and Bing

Before I look in detail at the reliable research resources with which you will need to become familiar, I wish to sound a word of warning. There is a great temptation, when you want to research someone, to simply put their name into Google and see what comes up. If you are really daring, you may also try Bing or Yahoo.

Prospect Research

Please do try to resist this urge when you first begin to qualify your prospects. I know it is quick and easy, but that is the danger. In your haste to qualify your prospects as quickly and easily as you can, you are in danger of treating the first results you find as the most relevant or accurate. But this ignores a fundamental fact about search engine results: *they are ranked in the order that the search engine's algorithms are programmed to order them*, not in the order that will necessarily bring up the most relevant or accurate results for you. Of course, the people behind these search engines will argue that they strive to make sure that their search engine *is* programmed to bring up the most relevant and accurate results, but if you are trying to satisfy millions of users with vastly different research needs, how likely it is that the algorithms are favourable to your particular search requirements?

You can minimise non-relevant results in Google and Bing by becoming familiar with the various symbols and words (or search operators) that allow you to narrow down your search and exclude irrelevant results. For example, when you use the minus sign in front of a word, the results will exclude that word. And when you put a phrase in quotes, the results will only include pages with the same phrase in the same word order as the ones inside the quotes. Just compare searching for the phrase **"Google hedgehog"** with the phrase **Google hedgehog** to see the difference quote marks can make. I do recommend that you become as familiar with the basic search operators as you can; it

Chapter 7 Qualification

will save you a great deal of time and effort in the long run. You can find the full list of operators for each search engine by using the following phrases:

Google search operators
Bing search operators.

Something else to be wary of with search engines is that the location of your computer and your previous search history can skew the results (for this reason I try to remove my location and delete or not record my search history, so that each new search is as neutral and objective as possible). Your search may also bring up various suggestions in the form of predictive text below the search window, which may confuse and confound your search before you have even begun. The search engine is trying to predict what you are searching for, which can sometimes be useful (if it brings up your prospect's name with a company name) but can just as easily throw you off (if it brings up a different person with the same name as your prospect and the company *they* work for). To appreciate how much this can throw you off, just imagine one of your prospects is called Richard Branson, but not that one. A search of his name will return a great many results, but (nearly) all of them will be for the wrong person.

I am not saying you should never use Google or Bing, but you should use them to access, and base your research on, the reliable resources I list below, and then you will greatly minimise your chances of being led astray by a general web search. Remember the old idiom 'a lie can travel half way around the world while the truth is putting on its shoes'. The internet is awash with lies and half-truths, reported on multiple different websites, so do not think that just because something appears many times it is accurate. Websites are like people: some are reliable, some less so, and some are to be avoided altogether. If you base your research on reliable resources, you should go a long way towards avoiding the unreliable ones or spotting them for what they are.

One obvious example of when you should use Google or Bing is to see if you can find any obvious support for your charity from those prospects who are not on your database. A quick and simple search with your prospect's name and your charity's name (or your charity's cause or with the names of other charities related to that cause) can often identify those who have expressed support for your charity or the cause it represents. Try the following combinations:

"John Doe" "[Your charity's name]"
"John Doe" "[Your charity's cause]"
"John Doe" "[Similar charities]"

These searches will bring up newspaper articles or interviews in which the prospect has expressed support for your charity or the cause it represents (or, just as importantly, if they have been critical of your charity). They may also bring up fundraising pages such as JustGiving, set up by someone to raise money for your charity, to which the prospect has made a donation.

Chapter 7 Qualification

7.3 Companies House

Companies House is responsible for registering and dissolving limited companies, registering the information companies are legally required to supply, and making that information available to the public. It is therefore the essential resource for company and director information. Depending upon the type of company, you may be able to discover a great deal about a prospect's assets, their current and past directorships (which will give you a good idea of their career and seniority), information about their shareholdings and whether the companies of which they are a director or shareholder are profitable or not.

As well as the Companies House website itself, there are various other online company and director databases. They all source their information from Companies House, but some have the advantage of providing information in a more convenient format. Much of the information they provide is free, but for more detailed information you will have to pay. The one I use most often alongside Companies House is called Company Check. Unlike Companies House, Company Check displays a convenient summary of a company's finances as well as several other summaries including a list of shareholders and parental and subsidiary companies. This can be especially useful if you want to get a quick idea of a company's finances without looking through several years' worth of annual accounts.

Prospect Research

Whichever company resource you use, the amount of information available to you will vary depending upon the size and type of company. For many companies, you will only find very limited financial information, and for others, no financial information at all. In such cases you will need to make a judgement based upon the company website and what other information you can find from an internet search. Even after all this, you may be none the wiser as to how much money the company is worth or what your prospect's shareholding may be worth.

But for other companies, especially larger companies, extensive financial information will be available. If the prospect is a director or shareholder of a public limited company (one that makes its shares available to the public), then it should be possible to get a very accurate idea of the prospect's salary (it will be listed in the annual report) or the value of their shareholding in the company (you can get the latest share price by Googling the company's name and share price, then simply multiply this by the number of shares the prospect owns).

For private limited companies, the share price will not be listed, but there are other ways to value a company and estimate what your prospect's shareholding is worth.

1. **Shareholder Funds (or Net Worth or Net Asset Value)**. This method is particularly appropriate if the company has significant tangible assets, such

Chapter 7 Qualification

as a property or manufacturing company. To get a very general valuation, you could just use the basic figure for shareholder funds in the company's annual accounts, but to be more meaningful (and vital if the information is available), this figure really must be put in greater context by looking at the profits or losses the company has made in the last few years (one year can be misleading), whether turnover is expanding or contracting, and how the sector in which the company sits is doing generally. If a company has shareholder funds of £10m and your prospect owns a 50% share, they own, theoretically, £5m worth of shares. But if the company has been making losses of hundreds of thousands of pounds for several years, and in a declining industry, will anyone want to pay them anywhere close to that £5m for their shares? Very unlikely. On the other hand, if the company has been making *profits* of several hundred thousand pounds over the last few years, and in an expanding market, the prospect will want, and be right to expect, much more than £5m for their 50% share of the company.

2. **Post-tax profits**. For those companies that do not have obvious tangible assets, you should use the company's post-tax profits to make a valuation. The general rule for unquoted companies (i.e. private limited companies and also public limited companies too small to be listed or quoted on the

stock exchange) is that they are valued at between five and ten times their annual post-tax profit. But this is a *very* general figure. A well-established company may expect to be valued at 15 or 20 times its post-tax profit compared to a relatively new company and one must also take account of previous years' profits or losses, whether turnover is expanding or contracting, and how the sector in which the company sits is doing generally. As a rule of thumb, ask yourself, how many years would I be willing to wait to see a return on my investment if I were to buy the company? If a company looks as though it will continue to make healthy profits for years to come, you may be prepared to pay (and the owners will certainly expect) many times the current post-tax profit value. But if the profits are up and down, you may wish for a return on your investment much sooner and so only be prepared to pay a much lower multiple of the post-tax profit value.

3. **Comparable Company Analysis**. This method is for those companies which you cannot value using either of the previous two methods. The basic idea is that you find one or more companies whose value you *do* know which are similar to your chosen company (similar finances and sector) and basically use the value of these other companies to estimate a value for your company. As with the other methods, this can only ever give you a

Chapter 7 Qualification

general figure, but in the end, that is all you need. Remember the DPA's stipulation that the data you process be relevant and limited to what is necessary. Pages of detailed financial information about a prospect's various directorships and shareholdings is unlikely to be either. A brief summary based upon general figures is more appropriate. To find similar companies to your chosen company I would use the following search string:

Mergers and acquisitions [industry sector]

In other words, for the construction industry I would search for **Mergers and acquisitions construction** and for the brewing industry I would search for **Mergers and acquisitions brewing**. This will bring up news stories related to companies in the same sector as your company which have been sold (and so for which you have an accurate value) and also – perhaps more importantly – will let you know which trade magazines and journals specialise in listing sales of companies in that sector. You can then search these journals for sales of companies that more closely fit your own. This is, I must admit, a more time-consuming valuation method than the previous two and can sometimes feel rather like looking for a needle in a haystack and so you may decide it is not appropriate if you are just trying to qualify a prospect.

Prospect Research

If you cannot find a company on Companies House, it may be that your prospect owns or works for a company that does not need to be listed (e.g. a sole trader). Another option is that the company trades under a different name to that by which it is generally known. Try looking on the company's website to see if they use a different trading name. If it is not immediately apparent from the company's home page (as it is with some companies) then look for a page marked as 'Privacy Policy' or 'Terms and Conditions', as such pages usually list the company's registered name.

When searching for a prospect on Companies House or Company Check it is best to use the prospect's full name, otherwise you may find yourself having to search through hundreds of directors with the same name and not know which (if any) is yours. Having a full name means you can separate John Mortimer Doe from the other people called John Doe. If you do not know your prospect's full name, then you may be able to find it using 192.com, as this often lists people by their full names, and you can search for them by surname only and postcode. You can also identify your John Doe by his date of birth, as Companies House lists the month and year of birth next to a director's name and Company Check allows you to filter your list of names by year of birth.

If you are having trouble finding someone on one of these websites, then use Google or Bing to search for them using one of the following phrases:

Chapter 7 Qualification

"John Mortimer Doe" [if you know their full name]
John Doe 1966 [if you know their year of birth]
John Doe NW3 2QX [if you know their address]

If the prospect is listed in Companies House, this should bring up the relevant page on the Companies House website, or on Company Check or one of the other websites that derive their data from Companies House. If it does not bring up any results for one of these websites, then it is unlikely your prospect is listed as a director in Companies House (or you may be misspelling their name?)

7.4 LinkedIn

LinkedIn, the leading business-oriented social networking website, is an invaluable resource. It has over 300 million members, each of whom has a profile, and many of whom list their full career history, as well as the university and school they attended.

Use the following phrase in Google or Bing to find prospects on LinkedIn:

"Jane Doe" LinkedIn

The quotes are important as you want Google or Bing to search for the exact phrase Jane Doe and ignore LinkedIn pages it finds with the words Jane and Doe, which may refer to, for example, the LinkedIn record of Mary Doe, who works for Jane Smith Ltd.

A LinkedIn profile can be a great source of information about your prospect, telling you not only who they currently work for, but very often who they worked for before and for how long. It can give you a good idea of their career progression (including non-directorship positions, which do not always need to be registered with Companies House) and allows you to estimate the level of wealth they may have. Some people also list outside interests, including charitable interests, which can give you an idea of how philanthropic they are and which causes they like to support.

Once you know the prospect's company, you can search for their name with the company name on Google or Bing to see if it brings up a company biography. And do check your database to see if the company itself already supports you. If the prospect does not yet support you, but their company does, this can be a way to engage them on a personal level (check with your Corporate department about the best way to proceed).

7.5 Property Value

On its own, knowing the value of your prospect's home can only tell you so much about their worth, unless the property is very expensive (£5m or more in London and the home counties, £1m or more elsewhere) or very cheap (less than £100k). A very expensive property, even if you allow for a mortgage, is a good sign of wealth, just as a very inexpensive property is (probably) a sign that there is not much

Chapter 7 Qualification

wealth, but for properties in between, you will need to view property value alongside any other wealth indicators you have been able to find and make your own judgement.

Property websites such as Zoopla and Mouseprice keep records of property sales going back several years, allowing you to learn what someone's house may be worth and possibly what they paid for it.

If you are unsure whether your prospect still lives at the address you have for him or you only have a partial address, you can check the electoral roll. I use 192.com to access the electoral roll, but if you are after a totally free service, BT's Phone Book provides name and address information as well as the person's phone number (assuming they are not ex-directory).

7.6 Biographies

As we saw in chapter 5, it is relatively quick and easy to use *Who's Who*, which is available without subscription through library membership.

Being listed is not itself a sign of wealth, but it is a sign that your prospect has been successful in some sphere of life and this success may have brought financial gain with it. Their career, seniority, directorships and any other wealth indicators will help you to decide whether they are a prospect or not. You should also note what their family situation is. Is the prospect single, married or divorced? Do they have children and if so, are their children still dependent upon them? A prospect who is single with no children will have more disposable wealth than one who is married with children at school or university.

192.com can also be used to identify spouses and children as it often has an age range for each of the people listed at an address. This only works for children old enough to register to vote (16 in England and Wales, 14 in Scotland) so any children under this age will not appear on the electoral roll.

ThePeerage.com is another valuable biographical resource, providing a genealogical survey of the peerage of Britain as well as the royal families of Europe. It can be very useful for researching titled families, although I should add a word of caution; sometimes it is a little unclear what the source of the information is.

7.7 Trustees of charitable trusts

In England and Wales, the Charity Commission's Register of Charities is the obvious resource to find out who is a trustee of their own charitable trust (a sign of wealth) or a trustee of someone else's trust (still good to know). Unfortunately, you cannot use The Office of the Scottish Charity Regulator to search for trustees, as they do not keep a register of trustees. Having said that, many English and Scottish charities are also limited companies, which means their accounts (including a list of their directors, i.e. their trustees) will be listed with Companies House. So when you check a

Chapter 7 Qualification

prospect's directorships on Companies House, do keep an eye out for companies that are also charities.

To search for your prospect in the Register of Charities, use one of the searches below (trustees are often listed on the Register of Charities under their full name, and so searching for this should bring up your prospect and not any other John Doe who may be a trustee of another charity. On the other hand, if he is listed merely as John Doe, then you will need to try the second search):

"John Mortimer Doe" charitycommission.gov.uk
"John Doe" charitycommission.gov.uk

If the person is a trustee, this search should find the relevant trust record on the Charity Commission's website (you will then need to click on the **People** tab to see a list of the trustees and confirm it is the right trust). If this does not find anyone then you could try the following searches:

"John Mortimer Doe" opencharities.org
"John Doe" opencharities.org

These searches actually bring up results from the website Open Charities, which is very similar to the Register of Charities (from which it sources its information). The helpful people who run the site also provide a link from the charity's page on their website to the same charity's page on the Register of Charities website, which can be very useful. Do be aware, though, that Open Charities is not updated as frequently as the Register of Charities, so do not rely on it without checking the Register of Charities itself.

A prospect with their own charitable trust is a definite indicator of wealth. Trusts over a certain size have to send annual accounts to the Charity Commission and these can tell you a great deal about the prospect's wealth and philanthropic interests. Many charitable trusts list the previous years' donations individually, which is ideal, but even if they do not, for all but the smallest trusts, you will be able to see their annual expenditure, which can give you some indication of the prospect's wealth.

If the prospect does not have their own charitable trust but is a trustee of another charitable trust, this is still very useful to know. Even if the trust does not list your charity's cause amongst its areas of support, do not be put off. Many charitable trusts leave aside a small proportion of their annual expenditure to spend on a few of the trustees' favourite causes, some of which may fall outside their official remit, and so you may be able to persuade your prospect to include your charity amongst these.

7.8 Other philanthropy

Hard evidence of philanthropy is difficult to find for most prospects, but many charities list major donors in their annual reports. Your other option is Google/Bing and the following searches:

"Jane Doe" "trustee"

Chapter 7 Qualification

"Jane Doe" "charitable"
"Jane Doe" "donation"
"Jane Doe" "Thank you" "donors"

It is quite rare to know exactly what someone has given to a particular charity, but you can often get a very good idea if a prospect is listed as a donor in a charity's annual report. Some charities do actually list major donors by gift band, which is very helpful in telling you (approximately) what each donor has given. More usually, they are listed by category (Bronze, Silver, Gold, Platinum is one common grouping, as is Friends, Partners, Benefactors, Patrons). But even then, you can conclude that someone who is in the Platinum category has a higher gift capacity than someone in the gold, silver or bronze. At other times, donors are simply listed alphabetically, with no indication of what each person's gift is. But you can still assume a gift capacity of £10k-£25k, assuming a £10,000 is the cut-off point, which is the norm for many charities.

If you want to get a more accurate idea of what this cut-off point is, you should check the charity's website. Charities are increasingly trying to attract major gifts by having a page dedicated to major donors, which will describe some of the significant projects for which they are seeking funding and possibly outline some of the benefits to being a major donor to their charity (personalised visits to services, meeting other donors or key charity personnel at special events, and so forth).

Prospect Research

To attract the right level of donor, these major donor pages often specify what level of gift they consider to be a major donation. Once you know this, you will know *at least* what level of gift the donors in their 'Thank you' list made.

I should mention at this point that although most major donations to charity are made by the wealthy, not all of them are. People of limited means do sometimes make one-off major donations to a particular cause or charity close to their heart. But for the most part, a large donation is a good indicator of wealth.

7.9 News archives

The importance of unencumbered investigative journalism is recognised by data protection legislation such that journalists do not have to adhere to the act in the way that you and I do. This means that their articles and interviews often go into a greater level of detail than any other research resource. If you cannot find out anything about a prospect, or you want to confirm something you have read elsewhere from an unreliable source, then you should carry out a search on a news archive.

As well as confirming what you already know, you may learn valuable information about a prospect not found elsewhere; about their career, their interests and hobbies, how they help their local community or favourite charities and, most importantly, what they think of *your* charity. In particular, you should carry out the following searches:

"John Doe" "Your charity"
"John Doe" "Your charity's cause"
"John Doe" "Similar charities"

I use the online newspaper archive NewsBank, available without subscription through library membership. NewsBank is a collection of 60 or so national and local newspaper archives dating back between 15 and 30 years, depending upon the newspaper, and is a very useful resource for prospect research. Many local and nearly all national newspapers also have their own online archives. Do also check your local newspaper's website as it may not be covered by NewsBank.

7.10 Due diligence

Working for a charity, we are bound by the *Charities (Protection and Social Investment) Act 2016* and the powers it gives the Charity Commission to regulate charities. Regarding major gift fundraising specifically, we must understand that the Charity Commission requires us to carry out research into our donors for the purpose of due diligence.

The Charity Commission has produced a series of documents under the title *Protecting charities from harm: compliance toolkit*.

Chapter 2, *Due diligence, monitoring and verifying the end use of charitable funds*, states:

Trustees must carry out due diligence checks on donors, beneficiaries and local partners and can also monitor end use of funds.

In the opening summary of Chapter 2, the document states:

A significant aspect of a trustee's legal duty to protect charitable assets and to do so with care means carrying out proper due diligence on those individuals and organisations that give money to, receive money from or work closely with the charity.

Further down the summary, under the section *What do trustees have to do for due diligence?* it states (my emphasis):

Charity trustees need to put effective processes in place to provide adequate assurances about the identity of donors, **particularly substantial donors**, and to verify this where it is reasonable and necessary to do so... It does not mean charities must question every donation or ask for personal details about every donor. Trustees are likely to need to carry out further due diligence and take steps to **identify and verify the identity of more significant donors** so they can assess any risks.

We therefore have a legal obligation to check those sources (Companies House, Register of Charities and newspaper and magazine articles) which will enable us to carry out adequate due diligence on our major gift prospects.

Chapter 7 Qualification

And as was discussed in Chapter 3, we should not underestimate the damage to a charity's reputation by accepting a major gift from someone with a genuine conflict of interests with your charity.

If the CEO of a company which employs child labour in Asia gives £10,000 to the local museum in the town where he grew up and also to a national welfare charity, it is the latter which is risking the greater reputational risk by accepting the donation without adequately checking the donor's background. It might be embarrassing to the local charity to have the gift publicised, but it would be devastating to the welfare charity, showing a serious lack of judgement which would undoubtedly put off other donors, both large and small, and no doubt cause some surprise and irritation amongst the charity's staff.

Carrying out adequate due diligence is vitally important, and the larger the donation, the more important it is. The exact cut-off point (£10k? £50k?) is for you to decide, but as soon as you start to engage on a personal level with a prospect, as soon as you move beyond the stage of communicating through appeal mailings and other mass-communication techniques, then you should start to think about due diligence for prospects with a donation potential above this level.

It is easy enough to check which companies a prospect is a director of on Companies House and whether those companies pose a potential conflict of interests. For each company, check who the other directors are (and which other companies they are a director of), who the main shareholders are (CompanyCheck is good for this) and also have a look at the company's website. Who are their clients? Are they involved in any areas of work, or in any countries, which might create a possible conflict of interests with your charity? You can also check on the Companies House Disqualified Directors Register whether they have ever been disqualified from being a company director and why.

If the prospect is listed in *Who's Who* then you can see who they have worked for and what their recreations are. If you are an animal rights charity, for example, and you see that your potential donor lists "Hunting, shooting and fishing" amongst his recreations, you may want to avoid any involvement with him.

One final check is to search for the person's name on Google or Bing (and also on NewsBank or other news archive, if you want to be really thorough), with the following search string (adding your prospect's name at the beginning):

"Firstname surname" controversy OR corrupt OR prosecute OR fraud OR "court case" OR embezzle OR scam OR con

Don't worry about having to type this search string each time you want to check a prospect; simply type it out once and press search and then bookmark the results page to your favourites (calling it *Due Diligence search* for example). Then, whenever you want to check a prospect, simply select the page *Due Diligence search* and this will bring up the saved search string. Simply type in your prospect's name at the beginning and hey presto! You are good to go.

Due diligence may seem like a lot of hassle, but it must be done. Especially if your charity has a policy as to who it will or will not accept donations from. And even if it does not have such a policy, you would be foolish not to carry out some level of due diligence. The bottom line is, if there are certain people from whom your charity does not want to accept donations, you need to make all reasonable checks before accepting a major gift from a new prospect, just in case that new prospect is one of those people.

7.11 Other resources

You may have noticed that I did not include Wikipedia in my list of biographical resources. The reason for this is that whilst Wikipedia can sometimes be wonderful for biographical information, it can also be very unsatisfactory. It is written and edited by a wide variety of people, with different skill-sets, knowledge and experience, so you cannot rely equally on everything it contains. Wikipedia articles are supposed to be sourced, so follow the sources if they are there, and make your own judgement as to how reliable they are. If there are no sources, try to confirm the information from a reliable source – or treat it with great caution.

Prospect Research

You should also be wary of websites that use automated methods to trawl the internet for biographical information and present it as if it was collated by a person. Such sites may contain valuable information but they can also be out of date with unreliable or unverifiable information. Again, try to confirm the information from a reliable source. Salary sites should also be treated with caution as many of them rely on self-reporting and so are completely unverifiable. Use them as a rough guide by all means, but check them against newspaper and trade journal articles about salaries or job adverts related to the job in question.

Even more unreliable are weblogs and other personal websites that do not source the information or opinions they contain. As before, look to confirm any interesting information from a reliable source.

A company's own website, on the other hand, is generally sound, but do bear in mind that for many companies, their website will show you what the company wants you to see. A company may be close to insolvency, but have a lovely, colourful, thriving website! Companies House will give a truer picture of the company's fortunes than any website.

In conclusion, when you come to qualify your prospects, it is the more reliable resources upon which you should base your research (Companies House, the Register of Charities, the electoral roll, BT's Phone Book, *Who's Who*, company annual reports and company websites) leaving the less reliable for any gaps or supplementary information.

Am I saying that I never simply chuck someone's name into Google to see what comes up? Of course I do, but I've been doing this for years and know what to look out for. I won't be taken in by a website containing detailed, but unsourced, information about my prospect. At least, I hope I won't! Everyone gets caught out now and then; the trick is to use reliable sources of information as much as you can to minimise the risk and always try to confirm information from questionable sources using a reliable source.

The particular research resources you will need to qualify a prospect, and the order in which you should use them, will really depend upon the information you have about the prospect in the first place. If you know from the information contained in your database that a prospect is a previous major donor, has a private bank account and is a senior company director, then there is little further qualification to be done and it may be enough to check that their career information is still current through Companies House or LinkedIn. If the only piece of information you have is that they have a private bank account, then you may need to check several different resources before being able to qualify them to your satisfaction. The important point to realise is that *you will not necessarily need to check each resource*. Once you are satisfied a prospect is capable of a major gift and will be likely to want to support your charity (or you can find no reason to suggest they

Prospect Research

would not) then stop and move on to your next prospect. *Do not go all the way through the list of resources.* Save that for the more extensive research you will need to carry out when you begin cultivating them.

Lastly, and most importantly, there is one resource which you must check each and every time you come to qualify a new prospect and that is your database. The more you can learn about your prospect before you look to the internet, the better; you may discover some valuable information about their ability or inclination to make a major gift, thus saving you the time and trouble of looking on the internet. Do you know their profession, job title, seniority or anything else to indicate their wealth? Have they supported you before and if so for how long and for how much? (The longer they have supported you and the larger their donations, the more likely they are to be inclined to make a major gift). How old are they? At the peak of their career? Retired? How many children do they have? Are their children still living with them or are they independent? (People tend to give more if they are no longer paying for their children). Have they attended any events and if so, how many and how recently? What level of communication have they had with your charity and how much information did they provide? (The more information they provided, the more likely they are to trust you and so want to support you.). The answers to these questions can help you determine to what extent the prospect has major gift potential.

Chapter 7 Qualification

If you have any filing cabinets of old correspondence, then check these too. Do not simply presume that all relevant information will have been added to the database by your predecessors. And as I said in chapter 4, you should also check your previous annual reports, supporter newsletters and any related magazines or printed material. They are all potentially sources of information about prospects; information which may not be on your database. And do not forget to run names past your more long-serving colleagues; they too may have pertinent information about your prospect which is not on the database.

7.12 Troubleshooting

There may be occasions when you can find out little or nothing about your prospect, despite all the resources at your disposal. And it may be that there is simply nothing to find; that is the case with some people, even people with money. If your prospect retired before widespread internet use and wasn't prominent enough to feature in the press or was not a company director (and so will not be on Companies House), then you are highly likely to draw a blank when researching them. But there are some other possibilities that you should consider...

- Check how the prospect's name is spelt. It is easy to misspell an unusual or unfamiliar name. Are you using their first name, when they use their second name, or using their full name when they go by a nickname?

- If a woman, do they go by their married name, their maiden name or a combination of the two? Professional women often continue to use their maiden name in business circles. Separated or divorced women may also revert to their maiden name.

- Is there an email address that you can check? Some people use a completely different name to their given name and their email address may reflect this (this is more common with actors and singers).

- Finally, pay attention when searching for foreign names. In some countries and cultures, the surname comes before the first name or the father's surname may differ from the mother's.

If you do not have a prospect's address, there are several steps you can take to find either a work or a home address.

If you know the prospect's full name or date of birth, check Companies House. This will provide at least one address, even if for some people it is a service (i.e. not home) address. Check this address with those on the electoral roll or BT's phone directory to determine if the person still lives there. Or you could check *Who's Who*. If they have an entry, it is likely to have a contact address and it may be a home address.

Chapter 7 Qualification

7.13 Conclusion

And now it is your turn. Beginning with your first list of prospects, you must go down the list, looking at each prospect in turn, using the research resources to help you identify the salary, shareholdings or other wealth indicators necessary to qualify your prospect.

Do, do, do keep a written record of who you have looked at and what you have found (either in the form of a qualification profile or in the specific fields of your database). If you wish, you can add the information you find to your database (especially full name and date of birth, email or telephone numbers, and also to correct outdated, incomplete or incorrect information) but remember we are at the qualification stage; anything more may slow you down. As you go down the list, mark those who are obviously wealthy, and also those who are clearly not (or for whom you can find no information) and leave the rest to come back to at a later date. At this early stage, you are aiming to identify the best prospects; the 'maybes' can wait until later in your fundraising campaign, when you are more confident and experienced in what you are doing and so more capable of making a sound judgement about who may be wealthy and who not.

It can seem daunting, I know, when faced with scores or sometimes hundreds of prospects all needing qualification, but take heart! The more prospects you qualify the more adept you become and the easier it will be. Take your time over the first few prospects,

Prospect Research

until you really get a feel for each of the resources and how best to use them. Better to take it slowly at first and really get a feel for each resource than to rush it and make mistakes; you will only pay for these later when you mistakenly approach a prospect who you should have rejected at qualification – or worse, ignore a wealthy prospect whom you should have identified.

There is one further tip I can offer, and that is to use the various research resources (especially Companies House) to carry out some research on one or two *known* millionaires. It is not hard to find them; just look in the Sunday Times Rich List or one of the other rich lists which one can find on the internet. Don't go for the ultra-rich people; their finances will take far too long to unravel and many will be off-shore, making them quite impossible for you to find. Rather, pick someone low down the Rich List. Pick someone, in particular, who is described in the Rich List as owning a company. Look them up on one of the Companies House websites, paying particular attention to the turnover of the company, the net asset value, the profit or loss it is making. All of this will help you to appreciate how the Sunday Times Rich List arrived at their wealth value and give you a better understanding of how to value people's assets.

Chapter 7 Qualification

Websites

Companies House: https://beta.companieshouse.gov.uk

Company Check: http://companycheck.co.uk

LinkedIn: www.linkedin.com

192.com: www.192.com

BT's Phone Book: http://www.thephonebook.bt.com

ThePeerage.com: www.thepeerage.com

Register of Charities: http://beta.charitycommission.gov.uk

Office of the Scottish Charity Regulator: www.oscr.org.uk

Open Charities: http://opencharities.org

Newsbank: various websites depending upon library membership

Disqualified Directors Register: www.gov.uk/search-the-register-of-disqualified-company-directors

8

Preparing for cultivation

8.1 Gift capacity

How do you estimate a prospect's gift capacity? There are three basic methods, although they can be combined and indeed should be where you are able to do so:

1. A figure based on one or more fuzzy wealth indicators.
2. A figure based on a proportion of their annual salary, when you have clear evidence of what it is.
3. A figure based on a proportion of their net assets, when you have clear evidence of what they are and not including their primary residence.

Fuzzy wealth indicators are those that tell you that the prospect appears to be wealthy, but with little or no further information than that. E.g. being listed on your database as a major donor, a private bank account holder, having a particular job title, living in an expensive property or having a second property or holiday home, being listed as a major donor in another charity's Annual Report (especially for several

Chapter 8 Preparing for cultivation

charities), having their own charitable trust or pledging a legacy.

Fuzzy wealth indicators are in contrast to the two, far more precise, wealth indicators of annual salary and known assets. In contrast to the fuzzy wealth indicators, these can give you a very good idea about a prospect's gift capacity, but you must realise that knowing that someone earns £500,000 a year or owns 50% of a multi-million pound company, still only *indicates* that they are wealthy *as we do not know what level of debt they may have* in the form of mortgages, loans, and other debts.

This is why prospect research specialists such as Prospecting for Gold, Factary, & Wealthwatch only provide wealth estimates within broad wealth bands (£1m-£5m, £5m-10m, £10m-£25m, and so on). For those prospects for whom you are able to provide a wealth estimate, I recommend you do the same. Given the way assets fluctuate in value, recording a prospect's wealth within a broad wealth band is far more realistic than using a fixed figure. And you simply don't need to provide a precise figure to estimate someone's gift capacity, especially as your gift capacity figures should also be in broad bands (£5k-£10k, £10k-£25k, £25k-£50k, £50k-£100k, and so on).

Determining gift capacity from fuzzy wealth indicators can be a difficult proposition and in many cases you will simply be unable to reach a precise figure. The mere fact that someone lives in an expensive property, has a second property, lives in a tax haven, has pledged a legacy or has an impressive job title, tells us nothing substantial about how *much* they can give, but only that they are more likely to be able to make a major donation. Even if you find someone on your database who is a Fund Manager with a London house worth £5m and a second home in France, this only provides a stronger indication of their ability to make a major gift, rather than telling you with any accuracy what level of gift they may be able to make.

But there are fuzzy wealth indicators which we *can* use to estimate gift capacity. Most obviously, if a prospect has given you a significant donation in the past then it is likely that they will have the capacity to do so again. But you should be aware that their circumstances may have changed since their last major donation. Are they still working or have they retired? Is there anything that has happened to them – a failed business or divorce, for example – which could significantly alter their gift capacity adversely?

If all you have to go on is one single donation to your charity, then I would use that as your guide for the appropriate gift capacity band. So, someone who has made a donation of £10,000 I would put in the £10k-£25k band if they are under 60 (i.e. their earning is likely to have increased since their donation) and in the £5k-£10k band if they are over 70 (i.e. their gift capacity is likely to have fallen with retirement). If they are aged between 60 and 70 then I leave it entirely up to you! If the prospect has made several large

Chapter 8 Preparing for cultivation

donations over a period of years, then I would use the largest donation as your gift capacity guide and if they have made several large donations in a single year, then I would use the combined annual total as your guide. Adjust both figures as necessary to take account of their changing circumstances since they last made their donations (i.e. increasing wealth or retirement).

If someone has a private bank account, then this gives us something to work with (a minimum level of investible assets or a salary). Fundraisers commonly assume a prospect's gift capacity to be 5% of their salary and to keep things simple, I tend to use the same figure to estimate gift capacity from investible assets. So, for someone who banks with Coutts (£500k in investible assets required) I would assume a gift capacity of 5% of £500k, i.e. £25k. This would put them in the £10k-£25k band or the £25k-£50k depending upon what else I know about them which may have a bearing on their gift capacity. If I have no other information, I'll err on the side of caution and put them in the lower gift band. If I have a figure for both investible assets *and* salary (as is the case with Bank of Scotland, Lloyds and Nedbank), then I'll go for a gift capacity somewhere between 5% of the asset value and 5% of the salary.

Being listed as a major donor on another charity's annual report can also give you a tangible gift capacity, as for most charities this indicates a donation of at least £5,000, and more probably £10,000. For some fundraising campaigns (such as members of Great

Ormond Street's Tick Tock Club or Patrons of the NSPCC's Full Stop campaign) it indicates a substantially higher donation (at least £100,000 in the case of Patrons of the Full Stop campaign).

If a prospect has their own charitable trust then you may be able to get a very, very good idea of their gift capacity and their philanthropic interests. Trusts over a certain size have to send annual accounts to the Charity Commission and many trusts list the previous years' donations individually, giving you a clear indication of the prospect's gift capacity. For those trusts which do not list individual donations, you will be able to see their annual income and expenditure, which can give you some indication of their gift capacity.

In contrast to most fuzzy wealth indicators, knowing someone's annual salary can give you a very good idea of their gift capacity. The downside to this is that you can only get reliable information about someone's salary for very few professions indeed. If your prospect is a director of public limited company, you will be able to find their salary in the company's annual accounts on Companies House. And if your prospect is a partner in a leading law firm, very reliable information regarding their salary can be found by searching Google or Bing with the following phrase:

[Company name] partner salary

This should bring up newspaper and trade magazine articles about equity partners' annual salaries. Equity

Chapter 8 Preparing for cultivation

partners are those who own a share of the company (and are liable for its failure) and share the profits after all expenses are met. They are in contrast to salaried partners who normally receive a fixed share of profits (sometimes with performance bonuses) by way of salary and their status is therefore somewhat more akin to that of an employee than an equity partner. Partners typically start as salaried partners and enter the equity after a certain period, which varies from firm to firm.

If your prospect is a partner in one of the leading accountancy firms, then you can find information about their salary by searching Google or Bing with the following phrase:

Accountancy Age top 50

This will bring up a link to the website *Accountancy Age* and their list of top 100 accountancy firms sorted by UK fee income. The information of interest to us is the **Fees per partner** column which gives you an idea of partner salary, albeit a very rough and ready one. Divide the fees per partner figure by three (one third for staff, one third for overheads, one third for the partners!), and that is your rough, averaged out, partner salary. Very rough, but better than nothing. If your prospect has not been a partner for very long, lower the figure. If your prospect has been a partner for 15 years or more, increase the figure.

For nearly all other jobs, the only available salary information will be unreliable. Salary sites in particular should be treated with caution as many of them rely on self-reporting and are completely unverifiable. You could use them as a rough guide, to check against newspaper and trade journal articles about salaries or job adverts related to the job in question, but then why not just use those more reliable sources and ignore the salary sites? I tend to avoid them.

One final point with regard to salaries. Gross salary figures do not take into account income tax, pension contributions, mortgage payments, private healthcare, school fees, and other loans or debts, all of which may take a significant chunk out of the gross figure. For example, someone on a salary of £1m will have to pay over £400,000 in income tax, thus considerably reducing their take home pay. And that's the easy part to calculate. If the prospect is divorced, they may be paying alimony, but who knows how much? And what about school fees? Three or four children at boarding school will not leave much change from £100,000. This is why we use the comparatively low figure of 5% of annual salary to estimate gift capacity.

For those prospects for whom you do not have any information other than one or two fuzzy wealth indicators, you will have to use your intelligence, and a bit of common sense, to make an educated guess as to their gift capacity. This may seem a bit hit and miss, but remember that we are looking for a general idea of what the prospect may be capable of giving and *not a precise figure as to what they will actually want to give to your charity right now*. In other words, do not confuse gift capacity with what I term *donation potential*, that is, the

Chapter 8 Preparing for cultivation

amount you are actually going to ask for there and then. As a general rule of thumb, for a one-off capital campaign you may want to ask close or right up to the gift capacity figure, as the prospect will understand that they are unlikely to be asked for another donation (at least, not for several years) and the gift is not going towards ongoing work, but for a stand-alone project. Perhaps a once-in-a-lifetime project. But for an ongoing fundraising appeal, with which you want to encourage and develop a relationship with the prospect, possibly over many years, you should consider asking for a lower first gift, with the aim of increasing your ask over the years. In other words, a prospect's donation potential may change even though their gift capacity remains the same. Research by the bank Coutts & Co tells us that a million-pound charitable gift comes on average after 6 previous gifts, so do not think you will be shooting yourself in the foot by asking a multimillionaire prospect for a first donation of £10,000 (or less), if that is the level of the project which you think will most appeal to them. If the prospect is suitably impressed with your charity, they will be happy to increase their donation over time. But asking for too large a gift at the beginning of your relationship may lead to disappointment.

Always remember that gift capacity will increase or decrease depending upon the individual prospect's circumstances. Are they retired or still working? Do they have any children at school or university? Are they heavily involved with any other charities? All of these factors and others will influence the size of gift they may want to make.

8.2 Inclination

Gift capacity on its own only tells you so much. A prospect may have the capacity to make a gift of £100,000 to your charity, but have absolutely no inclination to do so. You do not want to waste valuable time and effort trying to get a major gift from someone who has little or no inclination to make one. Initially at least, you must approach those most inclined to your charity, and then, when you have built up more experience and confidence, you will be much better prepared to approach those who may take a little more convincing to support you with a major gift.

How do you evaluate a prospect's inclination to support you? For prospects who have never supported your charity, I would start with the motivational factors discussed in Chapter 2, which tell us that someone will be more inclined to support your charity with a major gift if,

- They care about the cause with which your charity is involved. E.g. they donate to or volunteer at another charity with the same cause, or they have attended an event at that charity or they have publicly expressed support or admiration for your cause.

- They, or one of their family or close friends, had a personal experience which either brought them

Chapter 8 Preparing for cultivation

into direct contact with your charity or which should give them an affinity with your charity. E.g. they have mentioned the personal experience in a news article or interview or a friend or relative has.

- They know someone who works for your charity or who is already a major donor to your charity. E.g. they went to school or university with them, or worked with them (co-directors or trustees) or they were neighbours or just know each other socially.

- They grew up in, or now live or work in, an area in which your charity operates. E.g. they grew up in Liverpool, now work in London, but have a large residence in Cornwall, potentially linking them to all three locations.

Those are the best criteria to use for prospects who have never supported your charity. For those prospects that do support you, there are additional criteria:

- The greater their investment in your charity (the longer they have supported you, the more gifts they have given and the larger the gifts), the greater their inclination to support you with a major gift.

- The more they have volunteered for your charity, the greater their inclination.

- The more events they have attended, the greater their inclination.

But how do you compare someone who clearly cares about your cause with someone who knows one of your existing major donors and grew up in an area in which your charity operates? Which of them do you approach first?

There really is no right answer to this question, but one method employed by some (and I emphasise *some*) fundraisers and researchers is to use a points system. This allows you to be systematic and objective about how you rank your prospects, increasing the likelihood that you will approach the right prospects first. But there are two important caveats. First, you must realise that to give a score to someone's inclination is to give an objective and precise figure to something which is, to a certain degree, subjective and imprecise. Second, your scoring system must be kept up to date, otherwise it will be of little value, and that can add up to a lot of extra administration, especially when your pool of prospects begins to grow.

For prospects who have never supported your charity I would use the following scoring system:

	0 Points	1 Point	2 Points
Cares about the cause	No Evidence	Some evidence	Clear evidence
Experience or affinity	No	Friends or family	Personally or close family
Personal connection	None	Distant, acquaintance	Close, knows well
Location connection	None	Born or moved to area	Born or works in area

Chapter 8 Preparing for cultivation

For prospects who already support your charity, I would use the well-known RFM model (based on the Recency, Frequency and Monetary value of gifts received) and add a score for volunteering and events attendance.

	0 Points	1 Point	2 Points
Frequency of support	One-off donor	Multiple donor	Regular donor
Recency of support	More than 5 years ago	1 to 4 years ago	Within the last year
Largest gift	Less than £50	£50-£100	More than £100
Volunteered?	Never	Once	Several Times
Attended an event?	Never	Once	Several Times

The tables above should very much be seen as general guidelines to be tweaked or moulded to suit your own circumstances. In particular, you must adjust the recency, frequency and value scores to reflect the situation at your charity; a small charity which has only been fundraising for a few years will clearly need different values to a larger charity which has been fundraising for several decades. If you have the services of an IT or database team at your disposal, then you can ask them to create the RFM scores automatically; it is not hard to do and it can be an immense time saver compared to trying to calculate them manually, especially if you have a large number of prospects.

You may be wondering if you should score those prospects who already support you with the motivational criteria as well as the RFM score. You can do, but do be aware that a high RFM score shows a clear and tangible involvement *and investment* in your charity which indicates that they must care about your cause and that it is very likely they have had a personal experience which either brought them into direct contact with your charity or which has given them an affinity with your charity. I would therefore not worry too much *at this stage* about trying to find further evidence that they care about your cause or have some affinity with your charity (but if you discover such pertinent information when you are cultivating them, then do make a note of it). But it does make sense to score them for a personal connection or if they are connected to a particular location where you work.

8.3 Cultivation profiles

You are now at the stage of having a list of qualified, ranked prospects, all ready to be cultivated for a major donation. The next step is to carry out more in-depth research into your top prospects. I should stress at this point that the purpose of this further research is *not* to create an in-depth profile of the prospect, or to find out as much information about the prospect as you can (i.e. a 'full profile'), but rather to create a profile which

Chapter 8 Preparing for cultivation

will aid the fundraisers in their efforts to cultivate the prospect and solicit a donation from them. For this reason, I call it a 'Cultivation Profile'. When compiling this profile, you should focus your efforts on providing information which the fundraiser will find useful and beneficial in cultivating prospects *and* be mindful of your responsibilities under the DPA. Heed the words of the ICO: "You should not hold more personal data than you need. Nor should the data you hold include irrelevant details." Do not simply add information for information's sake.

I would aim to include the following information in a cultivation profile, some of which you will have found when you created the qualification profile:

- A summary at the top of the page to give a quick snapshot of why the person is a good prospect.

- Family information, including what their spouse does and if they have any children.

- Career information, in so far as it is *relevant* (i.e. providing a 30-year career history, with dates, is probably unnecessary).

- Philanthropic information (causes or charities supported, especially their own charitable trust).

- Gift capacity (or all known wealth indicators, if no gift capacity is possible).

- Their interests, hobbies or related matters, if they are relevant (e.g. if they indicate what sort of event the prospect may like to be invited to).

- Rationale for approaching (known to support a related charity or cause, their likely interest in a particular project, etc.).

- More detailed due diligence, if necessary.

To carry out this research you will need to return to the list of resources discussed in the previous chapter and make use of those you have yet to use or possibly look again in more detail at those you have used already.

On the following pages I have produced a sample cultivation profile. Note that I start the profile with a summary, and then lay the information out in a clear, logical sequence, which nicely leads up to the 'Rationale for Approaching' the prospect at the end.

Chapter 8 Preparing for cultivation

Cultivation Profile – Walter Dashwood

Summary/snapshot

- Walter Dashwood is the founder chairman of multimillion pound fund manager, Dashwood Capital.
- He and his wife, Candida, are founder trustees of The Dashwood Charitable Trust and they are both trustees of other charities.
- Key quote: "Pretty much everything I'm involved in relates to trying to make people as great as I am, which is not easy for most people."

Biography

- Walter Reginald Dashwood is a Chartered Surveyor who has worked in the property industry for 20 years. He is a member of the Royal Institution of Chartered Surveyors, the Worshipful Company of Chartered Surveyors and is a Freeman of the City of London.
- He was born 3rd October 1973 and was brought up in Burghfield, near Reading, before moving to Hampstead, where he lives with his wife, Candida, and their two children, Harry and Persephone.
- In 2012/13 he served as High Sheriff of the County of Greater London. High Sheriffs act as the Queen's representative on criminal justice at county level, supporting the judiciary and the police, and working closely with voluntary sector organisations.

Career

- Walter Dashwood is founder Chairman of Dashwood Capital, a Real Estate Fund Manager. Founded in 2005, it has invested in and manages some £600m of commercial real estate assets for itself and for private clients.
- Before founding Dashwood Capital, Walter was Managing Director and Senior Adviser of October Asset Management. October AM was originally set up to manage the finances of the multimillionaire entrepreneur Virgil Beardy. They started with about £50m of property in 1990, which had increased to £2bn when Walter stepped down in 2005.

Prospect Research

- Before joining October AM, Walter worked for various local authorities in a variety of property related positions and before that he worked in manufacturing and banking.

Philanthropy

- Very philanthropic. He estimates that he spends half his time managing the Dashwood portfolio and half his time on his various charitable interests.
- Founder trustee, with his wife, of The Dashwood Charitable Trust, set up in 2000. The other trustee is Montgomery Jewell, a solicitor with Jarndyce & Jarndyce. The charity is funded entirely by the Dashwoods and gives away around £400,000 each year to a variety of charitable organisations within its remit.
- Walter is also a trustee of The Royal Shakespeare Company, since 2000, and The Lyric Theatre, Hammersmith, since 2005.
- Candida is a trustee of Pancreatic Cancer UK, since 2003, and the Pelvic Radiation Disease Association, since 2010.

Past communication

- Walter has been a regular donor since 1995, giving £5 a month until 2005, when he raised his donation to £10 a month. He has been invited to several events but has yet to attend any.
- There has been one application to The Dashwood Charitable Trust, in 2009, but it was unsuccessful as we do not really fit within their areas of giving.

Wealth & Gift capacity

- Walter owns 50% of the shareholding in Dashwood Capital (the other 50% is owned by a private equity company). One standard (and crude) valuation of an asset management company is to value it at between 5% and 15% of the assets it manages, the exact valuation to depend upon a variety of factors. As it manages £600m of assets, this would put Dashwood Capital's value between £30m and £90m, and Walter's stake between £15m and £45m.
- He was an equity partner in October Asset management, and although the bulk of the money (and the initial investment) was provided by Virgil Beardy, the 60-fold increase in its assets from 1996 to 2005 meant that Walter's initial stake was worth £30m when he was bought out by Virgil.
- Although an exact figure is not possible, we can conclude with certainty that Walter is a multimillionaire, with wealth in the region of £30-£40m

Chapter 8 Preparing for cultivation

being the most reasonable. He would therefore easily be capable of making a decent 6-figure donation if he so chose (he is known to have given The Royal Shakespeare Company over £100,000 in both 2008 and 2009, through the Dashwood Charitable Trust).

Rationale for Approaching

- He is a current supporter, known to be wealthy and philanthropic.
- He clearly likes us but we do not fit in with the charitable trust so we need to find a way to get him involved without going via the trust.
- Not responded to any event invitations, so a personal approach may be more productive, linked to a particular project?

Due Diligence

- There is no evidence of Walter Dashwood being a director or shareholder in any company, nor of holding any opinions or supporting any groups, which would impact negatively upon [your charity]. No news stories arousing suspicion or concern were found when researching Walter Dashwood.

8.4 Conclusion

As I said in the introduction, major gift fundraising classically involves the five stages of Identification, Qualification, Cultivation, Solicitation and Stewardship.

I have taken you through the first two stages of this process and you should now be in possession of a list of major gift prospects ready to be cultivated in support of your fundraising appeal. Or, at the very least, you know what you need to do to create such a list.

I have tried my best to take you step by step through the necessary stages in identifying and researching prospects, but there are some things that cannot be taught; they can only be learnt through experience. With that in mind, I urge you to practise using the various resources and techniques described throughout the book. Let the old vaudeville joke be your guide:

"How do I get to Carnegie Hall?"
"Practice, practice, practice!"

It is difficult to put into words the feelings of relief, satisfaction and, finally, pure joy you will feel when you first get a major gift from someone *you* have identified. It is something to be savoured. This will come, just as long as you stay calm, stay methodical, and remember that Rome wasn't built in a day. Identifying and

Chapter 8 Preparing for cultivation

researching major gift prospects takes time, so take your time. Do it properly. And then you will reap the rewards.

Good luck to you!

Appendix – Privacy Statement

We use information that is already in the public domain (information that has been published in print or online) to identify high net worth individuals (i.e. millionaires) who may be interested in supporting our work with a major gift. These publicly available sources of information include Companies House, the electoral register, the phone book, the Charity Commission's Register of Charities, Who's Who, LinkedIn, company annual reports and articles in newspapers and magazines.

We do not use publicly available sources which we consider would be intrusive such as Facebook, Twitter, JustGiving, the Land Registry, online planning applications, or websites that are similar to these.

We also use information that is already in the public domain (information that has been published in print or online) to identify high net worth individuals who may be known to our existing major donors and so may wish to support our work with a major gift.

We also use various wealth screening techniques to identify high net worth individuals on our supporter database. These techniques are based both on publicly available information and information our supporters have given us voluntarily (e.g. where they live, who they bank with, what their occupation is).

Under data protection legislation, you have the right to object to your data being processed in this way. If you wish to opt out of being identified as a high net worth individual, please contact our Philanthropy Team.

Acknowledgements

I am very grateful to John Sauvé-Rodd, Emily Drayson and Ben Rymer for providing excellent and much needed feedback on earlier drafts of this book.

I am also very grateful to all the prospect researchers and fundraisers with whom I have discussed and shared best practice over the last 15 years, but in particular Adrian Beney, Helen Brown, Elly Bohme, Chris Carnie, Finbar Cullen, Becky Funnell, Matt Ide, Robin Jones, Andrew Thomas and Michael Triff. All of them have influenced the content of this book to some extent, but they bear no responsibility for its deficiencies.

I blame society for that!

About the author

Mathew Iredale has worked in fundraising since 1995 and in prospect research since 2000, working for such well known charities as Alzheimer's Society, Cancer Research UK, Great Ormond Street Hospital Children's Charity, Shelter and the Stroke Association.

He sat on the committee of Researchers in Fundraising from 2006 until 2012 and served as chairman in 2008 and 2009 and in 2012 he set up his own prospect research consultancy, The Prospect Research Toolkit, to provide freelance, consultancy and training services to charitable organisations.

He has twice spoken at the Institute of Fundraising's National Convention and was the expert speaker on research for the Directory of Social Change's major gift fundraising course, "How to win major gifts", from 2006 to 2008.

His first fundraising book, *Prospecting for Benefactors: how to find major donors to support your school*, was published in 2015. This was followed in 2016 by *Prospecting for Philanthropists: how to find major donors to support your charity*.